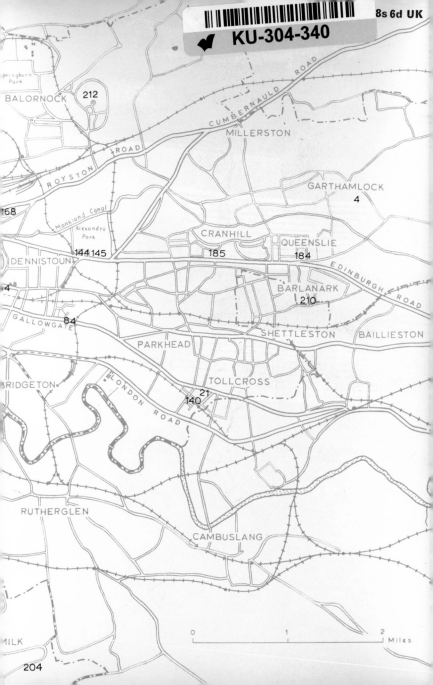

Glasgow at a Glance

Edited by **ANDREW McLAREN YOUNG**
and **A. M. DOAK**

Glasgow at a Glance

AN ARCHITECTURAL HANDBOOK

Collins   *144 Cathedral Street, Glasgow*

With contributions from
DAVID WALKER
R.W.K.C. Rogerson, J. Armstrong Lane,
Ronald McFadzean and **Roger Brunyate**

Introduction

The arrangement of this book is chronological rather than topographical. Beginning with the Cathedral (frontispiece, Nos. 1A, 1B), Glasgow's earliest building of importance, it follows the progress of architecture in what are now the city boundaries up to the present day (No. 217). This main section is followed (Nos. 218-25) by one entitled 'The Future', a kind of postscript on work in progress. There are two indexes: one of architects augmented with a little information about them, the other of buildings and streets. Maps on the end-papers should help the reader to find the buildings referred to. There is no table of contents; this paragraph acts as a substitute for one.

It is appropriate that the Cathedral should be the first building discussed in this book. From it, and from the venerated tomb of St. Mungo round which it is built, Glasgow derived its pre-eminence among the early settlements in the lower Clyde valley. Geographical factors favoured other places: Dumbarton was more easily defensible, and Paisley, Renfrew and Rutherglen— the last a senior burgh—were better placed in relation to the routes leading south. Govan, beside a ford at what was probably the head of navigation, appears for a time to have challenged Glasgow's supremacy, and some remarkable sculptured stones from its churchyard, which ante-date by several centuries any existing part of the Cathedral, are witnesses to a society far from barbarous. (The most important of these, the 'Govan Sarcophagus', is so interesting that, perhaps a little irrelevantly in an architectural guide, it is illustrated here as one of the region's earliest surviving works of art.) But Glasgow has grown and Govan is now part of it.

The 'Govan Sarcophagus,' now in Govan Parish Church.

Glasgow's expansion from the small medieval nucleus round the Cathedral was at first gradual. In 1451 it consolidated its position by becoming a university city—though it must be admitted that the early years of the College's life were not particularly distinguished. Growth, however, was considerably slower than in Edinburgh which, on the east coast, was much more accessible to the Continent. It was not until the opening up of the American and West Indian colonies that Glasgow, strategically located to exploit new conditions, came into its own. Real prosperity arrived when, in 1707, as a result of the Act of Union, the barriers against Scottish trade with the Colonies were removed. First came the Tobacco Era, with its scarlet-cloaked 'tobacco lords'; and, when as a result of the American War of Independence of 1775 this trade faltered, cotton—with a new merchant aristocracy—replaced it as Glasgow's chief source of wealth. The establishment of ship-building and heavy engineering, with which today Glasgow's name is nearly always associated, did not come till the intensive exploitation of the nearby coalfields in the mid-nineteenth century. In recent years too much dependence on these industries, which in their turn almost completely superseded cotton, has brought less prosperity than of old. But even the briefest historical survey of Glasgow shows a remarkable capacity for renewal. Such a process is now in operation; it is not, however, the function of a book on architecture to describe it.

Each phase of Glasgow's history has had its own notable buildings. There have, inevitably, been several sad losses—the pleasant and intimate seventeenth-century Old College (see No. 9) and two splendid Adam creations, the Assembly Rooms (see No. 13) and the Royal Infirmary, are among them. But Glasgow has never for long indulged in wholesale processes of vandalism; and, from the eighteenth century onwards, good and at times almost idiosyncratically individual architecture has been produced. In two styles at least Glaswegians can claim without boasting (for others have claimed it for them) that in invention and accomplishment their architects were ahead of any Scottish or English contemporaries. Two of them, Alexander ('Greek') Thomson and Charles Rennie Mackintosh produced work quite unmatched elsewhere in Britain. The great Thomson churches and terraces show that, at a time when the Gothic Revival was often ludicrously misusing noble style, a new and imaginative interpretation of classical architecture had particular relevance to urban needs. If Mackintosh, with a much smaller corpus of achievement, is even more famous it is because his is the wilder, more prophetic genius which, without disregard for the past, heralds the international architecture of the Modern Movement.

All this is well known to students of architecture in Glasgow and beyond its boundaries. Nowadays the reputations of Thomson and Mackintosh stand high. But perhaps less attention has been given to others: to William Stark, David Hamilton and John Stephen whose work, though neo-Greek, was never aridly so; to Charles Wilson (author of the incomparable Park Hill project), J. T. Rochead, John Burnet, John Honeyman, James Sellars and other near-contemporaries of Thomson who share the collective responsibility for some of the finest architecture and civic planning of the later nineteenth century; to the prolific and highly professional Sir John James Burnet; and to the younger James Salmon, Gaff Gillespie and other practitioners of the Art Nouveau whose work shows that Mackintosh did not exist in complete isolation. There is something about each of these, and many others, in the pages that follow. There is also a little about the patrons who made their work possible: the tobacco lords, the cotton manufacturers, the shipbuilders, the bankers, the businessmen, the public bodies and the churches.

But this book is not solely concerned with the past. Current achievements are recorded and future intentions described. For Glasgow is a living city and its architecture, no less than its industry and its commerce, must renew itself. It would, however, be foolish if in doing so it chooses to ignore the traditions that make it what it is. The old and the new can and ought to be made to live together.

To list everything of architectural merit was clearly beyond the scope of this book. All the really outstanding buildings are here but there are others of good quality that had to be excluded for reasons of space. In an anthology—and in a sense that is what this book is—there may even be inclusions less good than some of the absentees. We hope no one will ever try to justify an act of destruction by saying that his building is not in *Glasgow at a Glance*.

This book had its origin in a proposal made by Mr. Robert Ponsonby at a meeting of the Glasgow Advisory Council of the Commonwealth Arts Festival. Visitors, he thought, would welcome some kind of guide to the architectural wealth of a city so often wrongly described as drab and monotonous. The idea was given encouraging support; and, it was observed, the book's appeal might be as much to inhabitants as to visitors. Thanks to the Corporation of Glasgow and the Universities of Glasgow and Strathclyde, who have all generously helped to meet the costs of publication, a means was found of turning this proposal into reality.

Glasgow is fortunate in having a number of well-informed students of its architecture. Mr. David Walker is one of the most knowledgeable of them and, when a voluntary team of writers was recruited, he became an important member of it. His has been the responsibility for the eighteenth, nineteenth and earlier twentieth centuries—indeed, as the reader will note, considerably more than half the book. Mr. A. M. Doak, editor of the Yearbook of the Glasgow Institute of Architects, has helped in a variety of ways, and in particular with the modern section; in this he has had the co-operation of three professional colleagues, Mr. R. W. K. C. Rogerson, Mr. J. Armstrong Lane and Mr. Ronald McFadzean. The pages devoted to future developments were written by Mr. Roger Brunyate. Mr. Ronald G. Cant and Mr. Ian G. Lindsay have most generously permitted what almost amounts to plagiarisation from the descriptions of the pre-1700 buildings in their excellent little book, *Old Glasgow,* 1947. At different times assistance was given by Mr. H. C. S. Ferguson, Mr. T. C. Livingstone and Mr. Frank A. Walker. As editor my task, apart from the making of a few scattered contributions to the text, involved the co-ordination of all these efforts; with such willing colleagues it was a pleasant one.

For a long time Mr. Alfred G. Lochead has occupied a unique place among the historians of Glasgow's architecture. Everyone who has ventured into the field is in a large measure indebted to him. Though not directly involved he has kept a paternal eye on our efforts and has always been ready to answer, or find the answer to, any difficult question. Had this been the kind of book to be dedicated to anyone we should all have chosen Mr. Lochhead; under the circumstances we can only acknowledge how much we owe to him. Others, too, must be mentioned. It was Mr. Francis Worsdall who first discovered the authorship of the Suspension Bridge pylons; the knowledge of Mr. Alexander Smellie, of Professor William Smith and of Mr. Alexander Wright has been at our disposal; and the Corporation Architectural Department and the architectural firms whose work appears in the contemporary part of the book have given informative and courteous replies to what must have seemed an incessant bombardment of questions. To all we express our gratitude.

This is first and foremost a picture book with its text written as a commentary on the illustrations: without the photographs from which they were made it could not have existed. Many of these are new, taken specially for this book. We are particularly grateful to Mr. Robert Cowper of the Glasgow University Department of Fine Art and to Miss Catherine Cruft and the photographers of the Scottish National Buildings Record who, between them, took on the responsibility for the major part of this undertaking. Their task, however, would have been still greater had it not been for all the other contributions from photographers both amateur and professional—it should be recorded that in not a single instance were we asked to pay a reproduction fee. In listing opposite the sources of our illustrations we take the opportunity of thanking all those who supplied them:

Messrs. T. & R. Annan (Nos. 1B, 2, 3, 10B, 26A, 58, 64, 67, 89, 98, 102, 146B, 146D, 146L, on the cover and on p. 6) ; the *Architects' Journal* (49B, 153B, 160) ; the British Council (146 I) ; Messrs. Bryan & Shear (146A, 146F) ; Mr. D. C. Buwalda (101) ; the Glasgow Chamber of Commerce and the late Mr. D. L. Stewart (10A) ; Dr. Ronald Falconer of the B.B.C. (1C, 110, and on the cover) ; the *Glasgow Herald* and its Art Editor Mr. A. M. Burnie (7, 11A, 24, 26B, 30, 52, 92, 103, 104B, 127, 129) ; Mr. John J. W. Goodchild (146E) ; Mr. James C. Howie (5, 13, 29, 65, 119, 166) ; Mr. Bedford Lemere (146J, 146K) ; Mr. Thomas Mann (146G) ; Mr. Hamish Miles (164) ; Miss Judith Pritchard (53) ; Miss Flora Ritchie (20) ; the Scottish Development Department and Mr. Douglas Scott (44, 57, 128, 152, and on the cover) ; the *Scottish Field* and Mr. George B. Alden (14, 18B, 36, 66, 68, 72, 111B, 150) ; the Scottish National Buildings Record (4, 6, 12, 16, 18A, 19, 22, 25, 27, 28, 32, 33, 35, 40, 42, 45, 46, 49A, 50, 63, 69, 71, 78, 82, 85, 86, 90, 94, 105, 111A, 113-5, 117, 124, 130, 135, 136, 138, 139, 142, and on the cover) ; Scottish Studios (9A, 9B, 39, 88C, 112, 154, 171, 178) ; Dr. Neil Spurway (161) ; Mr. Wilson Steel (146C, 146H) ; Studio Seven (51, 107, 116, 141, 153A, 198) ; Mr. William Thomson and Mr. Thomas Walsh (11B, 60, 62) ; University of Glasgow, Archives (17) ; University of Glasgow, Department of Fine Art and Mr. Robert Cowper (1A, 8, 15, 23, 31, 34, 37, 38, 41, 47, 48, 54-6, 61, 73-7, 83, 84, 87, 91, 95-7, 99, 104A, 106, 108, 109, 120, 121, 123, 125, 126, 131-3, 137, 140 143-5, 149, 151, 155-9, 162, 163, 165, 167, 168, 174, 176, 196, and on the cover) ; University of Glasgow, Mackintosh Collection (147A, 147B, 148) ; University of Strathclyde, School of Architecture (78, 80, 81, 88A, 88B, 93, 100, 134) ; Mr. David Walker (21, 43, 59, 70, 122, 175). Photographs have also been provided by the owners of some of the buildings illustrated (118, 170, 172, 177) and by the architects of others (169A, 169B, 173, 179, 180-5, 186, 188, 189-91, 192-5, 197, 199-225).

We also gratefully acknowledge the loan of blocks from the Glasgow Institute of Architects (14, 40, 177, 187-91, 201) ; from Her Majesty's Stationery Office (44) ; and from the *Scottish Art Review,* through its editor Miss Isabel Mackintosh (1B, 18B, 64.)

Finally, for a diversity of tasks in the preparation of the book, we must thank Mrs. Judith Gillis, Miss Pearl Howden, Miss Stella Smith, Mrs. Grace Watson and Miss Caroline Young.

ANDREW McLAREN YOUNG

The Art Nouveau coats-of-arms of Scotland and Glasgow are adapted from two beaten metal reliefs on the exterior of a building by the younger James Salmon at 24 West Regent Street.

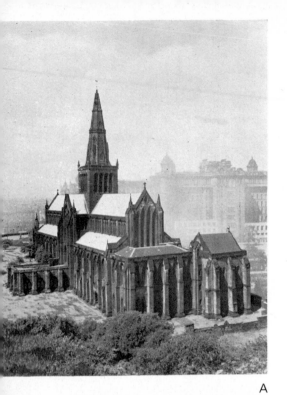

A

B

1. GLASGOW CATHEDRAL. Cathedral Square. Early 13-C onwards. Third on site, dedicated to St. Kentigern or Mungo. In Gothic 'First Pointed' style; largely completed, except for nave, by end of 13-C.; remarkable for consistency of design though chapter-house and central spire belong to early 15-C. 8-bay nave, 5-bay choir (now set out for Presbyterian worship) with eastern chapels; transepts extend only to line of aisles except where the later Fergus aisle prolongs south transept at crypt level; dramatic crossing with steps rising several feet to choir and others descending at both sides to spacious and elaborately vaulted lower church containing St. Mungo's shrine which, because of the slope of the ground, receives light through windows at east end. The whole structure, timber roofed, marked by a severe elegance. Two dissimilar western towers removed as a stylistic 'improvement' in 1846-8. Stone choir screen of late 15-C.; glass mostly recent, replacing vast Victorian-German scheme; Father Willis organ, revised, in minimal casework.

Frontispiece *The Crossing*
A. *View from the South-East*
B. *Lower Church with St. Mungo's Shrine*

2. CROOKSTON CASTLE, Pollok. Late 14-C. Massive rectangular main block with remains of square angle-towers; staircase to main hall in thickness of wall. Built for an ancestor of Mary Stuart's Darnley and successively owned by the Earls of Lennox and the Maxwells of Pollok.

3. PROVAND'S LORDSHIP, Castle Street opposite Cathedral Square. Plain crow-stepped building, 1471, with wings added behind, 1670 (restored, 1906). Built as clergy house of St. Nicholas's Hospital and became the manse of the Prebend, or Provand, of Barlanark (see PROVAN HALL No. 4).

4. PROVAN HALL, Garthamlock. North block round courtyard, with crow-stepped gables and round tower, 16-C.; entrance gateway, dated 1647; south block, with staircase and panelling, 18-C. Originally part of the Prebend of Barlanark (see PROVAND'S LORDSHIP No. 3).

5

6

8. HAGGS CASTLE, 100 St. Andrew's Dr. 1585 (according to panel over former main doorway); repaired twice in 19-C., when bow front, turret and wing at rear were added. Ornate castellated style; intricate carved detail over the now blocked up main door and on the dormers. (*left*)

9. Relics of the OLD COLLEGE, now at Gilmorehill. Original building, mid 17-C. (possibly from the designs of *John Mylne*), demolished to make way for a railway goods yard. The present University gatehouse, PEARCE LODGE (A), by *A. G. Thomson*, 1888, is a composition of fragments from the main façade. The LION AND UNICORN STAIR (B), 1690, stood in the Outer Quadrangle; it has now been made to turn left instead of right.

5. TRON STEEPLE, Trongate. Worked on 1593-5, completed 1630-6. All that remains of the Tron Church which was burned in 1793 and rebuilt a little apart. The 4-centred ground-floor arches by *John Carrick*, 1855. Spire perhaps derives from the Cathedral (No. 1).

6. TOLBOOTH STEEPLE, Glasgow Cross. 1626. Seven-storey tower, with imperial crown and small carillion, survivor of the demolished New Tolbooth or Town House. A thorn in the flesh to traffic-flow-improvers its existence has been threatened. (The adjacent Mercat Cross, by *Edith Burnet Hughes*, 1930, replaces one removed in 1659.)

7. MERCHANTS' STEEPLE, Bridgegate. Finished 1665. The 'Bri'gate Steeple' survives mid 17-C. Guildhall and Hospital, and protrudes through roof of 19-C. Fish Market (No. 50). Charming compound of Gothic and Renaissance features.

7

A **9** B

A

10. ST. ANDREW'S PARISH CHURCH, St. Andrew's Sq. 1739-56. *Allan Dreghorn*. Mungo Naismith, master mason. General design and plan based on Gibbs's St. Martin's-in-the-Fields, London, but rather smaller in scale; treatment decidedly Scottish with a slim steeple (A) in the Glasgow tradition. The magnificent interior plaster work (B) in the rococo manner is by Thomas Clayton who worked at Drum, Blair Castle and Hamilton Palace; mahogany gallery fronts. Siting of the church initiated the characteristic Glasgow pattern of squares encircling major pieces of architecture.

B

12. ST. ANDREW'S-BY-THE-GREEN, 33 Turnbull St. 1750-51. *Andrew Hunter*, master mason (no architect's name mentioned in minutes). Glasgow's oldest Episcopal church built as such, and still in use—though precariously in path of the proposed ring road. Galleried interior; organ by Donaldson of York, 1795, formerly in Glasgow Cathedral (installed here 1812). Hunter, a Seceder, was excommunicated for building the church.

11A

11B

12

11. POLLOK HOUSE, Pollokshaws. Designed by *William Adam, Sr.* (d.1748); completed by his son *John Adam*, 1752. Main part (A) facing White Cart river almost unadorned, but good proportions. Entrance hall, wings, terrace and garden pavilions, in harmony with main building, added by *Sir Rowand Anderson*, *c*.1900. Elegant 18-C. bridge. Stable block, mid 18 C., incorporates a fragment of the 14-C. house and a fine gateway (B) of *c*.1600; pediment above, with its gothick arch, appears to be a late 18-C. addition. (House contains remarkable collection of pictures including two El Grecos and several Blakes.)

13. McLENNAN ARCH, Charlotte St. From *R. & J. Adam's* Assembly Rooms, 1792-6; re-erected here, 1893. Though the task was done without any adventitious 'improvements' it is sad that the original building had to go. Behind the arch is Our Lady and St. Francis School by *Gillespie, Kidd & Coia* (No. 211).

14. TRADES HOUSE, 85 Glassford Street. Completed 1794. *Robert Adam.* Façade virtually intact, but extensively remodelled within; the single bays to left and right and unhappy architrave inserted into the doorway are additions. Adam's other principal work in Glasgow, the Infirmary, survives only in faded photographs.

15. ST. GEORGE'S TRON CHURCH, Buchanan St. 1807. *William Stark.* Exemplifies the catholicity of Stark's taste and his predilection for experiment: treatment of lower part of tower shows study of Hawksmoor and upper part Wren, both in 1807 stylistically out of fashion. The obelisks were to have been statues which would have accentuated the Baroque character of the composition. Crown top a possible progenitor of Thomson's St. Vincent St. Church (No. 64). Stark's masterpiece, the Lunatic Asylum, a radial plan building, long ago destroyed; his old Hunterian Museum also only a memory.

16. 42 Miller St. 1775. Built by *John Craig*, wright. Only survivor of many such houses in Miller St. and other new town streets. Pediment appears to have been intended for sculpture, doubtless deferred in consequence of the builder's financial embarrassment. Clumsy mansard a much later addition.

17. Former OLD COLLEGE STAFF RESIDENCES, 169-177 and 179-183 High St. 1793-5. *James Adam.* Characteristic late Adam design with 'Prince of Wales' order. Nearer block altered. Now sadly dilapidated and in path of ring road; their stonework, however, in good order and capable of re-erection.

16   **17**

18. Carlton Place.
Begun 1802. *Peter Nicholson,*
a migrant architect who left
Glasgow while work was still
in progress. Impressive terrace
(A) facing the Clyde; intended
as part of a never-completed
larger development promoted
by John Laurie; first Glasgow
attempt at organizing a whole
street into a symmetrical
composition. Laurie's own
LAURIESTON HOUSE, 1804,
in nearest pedimented centre,
has one of the most elaborate
domestic interiors (B) of the
period executed, it is said, by
Italian craftsmen—but, at this
time, there was native work of
equally high quality. The line
of the terrace marred by an
ugly Edwardian insertion;
greatly improved by a recent
Civic Trust operation; most
sensibly left, as a haven of
history, in the new Gorbals
redevelopment scheme.

B

19. HUTCHESONS' HOSPITAL,
158 Ingram St. 1802-5. *David Hamilton*.
In Hamilton's early style, a compound of
late Adam, Louis Seize and early Soane
elements; steeple a traditional Scots
feature for such buildings. Statues of
the Hutcheson brothers are those made
in 1649 by James Colquhoun. Interior
redone by the second *John Baird* in 1876.

20. AITKENHEAD HOUSE, King's Park. 1806,
1823 and 1828. Work at latter dates, if not all,
by *David Hamilton*. Centre block was, of course,
first part built but may have been re-cast later.
Staircase had a magnificent coffered dome
continuous with its pendentives; rest of interior,
always interesting, shows markedly the influence
of Sir John Soane. Now a municipal branch
museum.

21. TOLLCROSS CENTRAL CHURCH, 1088 Tollcross Rd. 1806. *John Brash*. A simple vernacular design which although long absorbed in the city preserves its country church atmosphere. Tower and spire (1834-5) unusual feature for a Secession (Relief) Church.

22. GREYFRIARS-ALEXANDRA PARADE CHURCH, 182 Albion St. 1821. *John Baird*, the elder of two architects of that name, then aged 23. Originally a Secession church and the first to be architecturally self-conscious; finely detailed portico; interior galleried and substantially unaltered. Now deserted and possibly to be demolished. (*centre*)

23. JUSTICIARY COURTHOUSES, Saltmarket and Clyde St. 1807-14. *William Stark*. Rebuilt 1913 by J. H. Craigie of Clarke & Bell. First large Greek Doric portico in Glasgow and, when designed, the first in Britain; original scheme also comprised municipal offices and prison. Craigie's thoroughgoing reconstruction, the last of several alterations, leaves the façade only an approximation of the original and omits the channelling which gave it a French flavour.

24. Blythswood Square. 1823-9.
Unknown. Glasgow's only square in
the contemporary Edinburgh manner
though the treatment, especially that
of the plain upper floor, is more
reticent. The builder responsible for
most of the work went bankrupt. At
No. 5 an inserted doorway by *Charles
Rennie Mackintosh*, 1908.

25. VIRGINIA BUILDINGS,
37-53 Virginia St. 1817.
Unknown. Best street architecture of
this vintage to survive intact—house
at 49-53 especially fine.

A

B

26. STIRLING'S LIBRARY
(formerly ROYAL EXCHANGE),
Royal Exchange Sq. 1828-30.
David Hamilton. Started life as the
Cunningham mansion, later
occupied by the Royal Bank. In
1827 the bank moved to new
premises (No. 28) and sold off the
mansion which Hamilton
economically left as part of his
monumental design (A). The rich
Graeco-Roman interior (B) shows
characteristic Hamilton touches
such as panelled pilasters and
continuous mouldings round the
windows. The main building,
thanks to sensitive adaptation by
Glasgow Corporation, is intact,
but parts of the surrounding
square, by Hamilton and his
son-in-law *James Smith,* are
badly in need of restoration (this
old photograph gives an idea of
what has been lost). Statue of
Wellington is by Marochetti, 1844.

27. 151-155 Queen Street. *c.* 1834. Style of *David Hamilton*. Built for Archibald McLellan, whose important art collection formed the nucleus of the civic art gallery; this no doubt explains its much more than average quality. Upper windows and pilastrade threaded through giant order at first floor are typical of Hamilton at that date.

28. ROYAL BANK OF SCOTLAND, Royal Exchange Sq. *c.* 1826-7. *Archibald Elliot*, but whether a posthumous work of the elder or by the younger, who practised in London, is not clear. Good example of the contemporary Edinburgh manner. The Buchanan St. frontage added by *Charles Wilson,* 1851-2; interior rebuilt by *Peddie & Kinnear,* 1872.

29

30

29. CUSTOM HOUSE, 298 Clyde St. 1840. *George Ledwell Taylor* of London. Attractive neo-Greek design with finely sculptured coat-of-arms; surprisingly modest in scale compared with those in Greenock, Leith and Dundee. Taylor is chiefly remembered for his chatty memoirs, 'Autobiography of an Octogenarian Architect', and as co-author, with Cresy, of a book on the architecture of Rome.

31. ST. ANDREWS R.C. CATHEDRAL, 172 Clyde St. 1816. *J. Gillespie Graham.* The first serious attempt at Gothic Revival in Glasgow with a neo-perpend-icular 'college chapel' front and plaster vaulted interior. Unfamiliarity with techniques of gothic building contributed to its then enormous cost of £16,000.

32. ST. DAVID'S (RAMSHORN) CHURCH, 98 Ingram St. 1824. *Thomas Rickman* of Birmingham. Sited, in conformity with a pattern common in the first new town area, as a focal point on the axis of Candleriggs. T-plan with undercroft and front tower; interior plaster vaulted. Rickman had abandoned medicine for the study of the Gothic style and was gradually drawn into architectural practice; though himself a Quaker he usually built for the Church of England.

30. WESTERN CLUB, 147 Buchanan St. 1840-1. *David* and *James Hamilton.* Best example of Hamilton's late, very experimental phase. Great consoled attic-cornice is Italian, but other features are peculiarly Hamilton's —the square column porch and the balconies with their lush Graeco-Roman details (drawn by *J. T. Rochead*). *John Honeyman* extended the St. Vincent St. frontage in 1871. Note how, right, John Burnet continued the cornice line in his Gothic Stock Exchange (No. 98).

33. BRITISH LINEN BANK, Queen and Ingram Sts. 1840. *David* and *James Hamilton*. Here as at the Western Club (No. 30) Italian Mannerist details are in evidence. The somewhat bizarre upper floors were added— surprisingly—by *Salmon & Gillespie*, 1904; corner dome recently taken down.

34. LANGSIDE PUBLIC HALL 1 Langside Ave. *John Gibson & Macdougal* of London, 1847 re-erected on present site, 1902-3. Originally the National Bank in Queen St. with a fine square of business chambers round it. An early work of Gibson who spent nearly all his life building splendid Renaissance edifices for the National Provincial Bank in England. The task of re-erection carefully done with no exterior change.

35. COUNTY BUILDINGS AND COURTHOUSES, 40-50 Wilson St. 1844. *Clarke & Bell.* Winner in competition; established Clarke & Bell in Glasgow. Central part to Candleriggs, formerly Merchants' House, was built concurrently; northern section to Ingram St. was built in 1871 and unhappily reconstructed later. Both central and north sections have suffered from ill-considered repairs but that in Wilson St. is still intact.

36. Claremont Terrace. 1842 and 1849. *John Baird I.* Centre house, originally a free-standing mansion, was first part built. The terrace continued the development of the Woodlands area begun by George Smith of Edinburgh, with Woodside Crescent and Terrace from 1831 onwards.

37. Kirklee Terrace. 1845. *Charles Wilson.* First of the Gt. Western Road terraces, crisply Italianate in style. Wilson, David Hamilton's pupil (articled in 1827, chief draughtsman by 1830s), nearly always aimed at economy of means while his master invariably sought richness of effect. Here his personal style has not quite reached maturity.

38. CHEAPSIDE BONDING COMPANY WAREHOUSE, Cheapside St. and Piccadilly St. 1804-6. *Boulton & Watt.* Wm. Creighton, resident engineer and draughtsman. Originally Houldsworth's Cotton Mill; the most impressive monument of early industry in Glasgow. A massive fireproof construction (224 x 39 ft.); brick built with cast iron frame and brick arches; six storeys and attic flat; 3-aisle plan; headroom, except at attic, only seven foot six. The stout columns were fitted for steam heat. Pilastered exterior an early attempt at bringing dignity to industrial design.

40. BUCK'S HEAD BUILDING, Dunlop and Argyle Sts. 1849 and c. 1864. *Alexander Thomson*. At the earlier date buildings were erected at the rear of the Buck's Head Hotel, 'Greek' Thomson's first large job. Revolutionary conception with giant pilastrade directly glazed at the upper level. This, though Thomson almost certainly did not know about it, had been done by Isaiah Rogers in Boston in 1843; Thomson was almost certainly the first in Europe. In the later corner block, replacing the hotel, external cast-iron work replaces much of the masonry.

39. CROWN ARCADE, 31-35 Virginia St. *c.* 1819, reconstructed mid century. *Unknown*. Originally the Tobacco Exchange and still with an aura of the Tobacco Era. Window over door at far end said to have been auctioneer's box. Timber architecture, once applied to façade, now but an after image on a plain wall. (*left*)

41. 81 Miller St. 1849-50. *James Salmon I*, the eldest of an architectural dynasty. Though Wylson's Canada Court in Queen St. was the first of the great Victorian warehouses it was far surpassed architecturally by Thomson's Buck's Head building (No. 40) and this well-designed one for Archibald McLellan, the great art collector. (*right*)

42. GARDNER'S ('THE IRON BUILDING'), 36 Jamaica St. 1855-6. *John Baird I* in conjunction with R. McConnell, an ironfounder who held structural patents. The spans between the main structural piers are wide for their time with framed girders of wrought and cast iron. Baird's successor, James Thomson, again with McConnell, built another at 217-221 Argyle St., but, there, the iron is treated less frankly—more like stone.

43. 30-34 Jamaica St. 1854. *John Honeyman.* A late example of the Venetian phase keeping company worthily and harmoniously with Iron Building (No. 42) seen on left. Its neighbour on right, authorship unknown, also of considerable interest but has suffered from unhappy first floor alterations and excrescences.

44. 37-51 Miller Street. 1854. *Alexander Kirkland.* One of the most extraordinary buildings ever to be erected as a warehouse with the usual plan turned inside out—probably as much for better daylighting as spectacular display. Venetian style allows for large glazed areas and deep recessions compensate for reduced sunlight. Doubtless intended to eclipse No. 81 in same street (No. 41). The architect, later Commissioner for public buildings in Chicago, died in Portland, Oregon, 1901.

45. 44 James Watt St. *c.* 1863. In a street containing several splendid old tobacco warehouses this is the finest. Note the integration of first and second floor windows. Iron columns are used but the floors are not fireproof.

46. SUSPENSION BRIDGE, Custom House Quay to Carlton Pl. 1851, reconstructed 1871. *Alexander Kirkland* (pylons), *George Martin* (engineering). Footbridge of 414-ft. span. The pure Greek of the pylons, in form of triumphal arches, unusual in Kirkland's œuvre. The hope of the Trustees who built it that its cost would be paid off by pontage was never realised. (The only other Clyde bridge of architectural merit is Victoria Bridge by John Walker, 1851-4.)

47. CA D'ORO, 120-36 Union St. and 41-55 Gordon St. 1872. *John Honeyman*. Originally a furniture warehouse. Upper floors cast iron fronted and comparable in merit with Gardner's (No. 42). Unfortunate mansard by *J. Gaff Gillespie*. (*centre*)

48. KIBBLE PALACE, Botanic Gdns. *c*.1860; re-erected here 1873. Originally built at Coulport by *James Kibble,* an engineer, at the cost of £15,000 (say £100,000 in today's money). Despite the legend linking it with Paxton it seems certain that Kibble alone was responsible. Inside, amid tropical vegetation, are dazzlingly white Victorian marble statues by Hamo Thornycroft, W. Goscombe John et al. (*below*)

49. Former RANDOLPH ELDER ENGINE WORKS, 13-23 Tradeston St. *c.*1860. *William Spence.* Now a seed warehouse. Once the birthplace of much Scottish industry and, architecturally, expressive of its purpose—its vast scale indicated by the foreground cars (A). The 'Egyptian' features have been compared with Thomson's and Stephen's but the style of the Loch Vennachar sluice-house engineer, James Bateman) is closer. Inside (B), iron stanchions and massive brick piers support immense built up timber beams.

B

50. FISH MARKET, 64-76 Clyde St. 1873. *Clarke & Bell.* A late work of the original founders of the firm using de l'Orme's French order; an elegant feature of the river front. Interior utilitarian with large cast-iron column hall.

51. Former ST. MATTHEW'S BLYTHSWOOD CHURCH, 256 Bath St. 1849-52. *J. T. Emmett* of London. First example of 'Tractarian' Gothic in Glasgow—surprisingly for an Independent congregation—and first of the tall spires which once dominated central Glasgow's skyline. The finest of the few survivors, its future is in real doubt.

52. Former CATHOLIC APOSTOLIC CHURCH, 340-362 McAslin St. *A. W. N. Pugin* and *James Salmon II*. The real authorship not revealed until 1907 on completion of James Salmon II's additions of narthex and north aisle. Good minor example of the work of the great Pugin.

53. ST. JUDE'S FREE PRESBYTERIAN CHURCH, 278 West George St. *c.* 1840. *John Stephen*. Very Greek in inspiration and an interesting forerunner of 'Greek' Thomson's work; great doorpiece, albeit of Greek precedent, is of a type Thomson was to make peculiarly his own; heavy block pediment and thin pilasters also point forward to him. The peristyle now built up (see inset from old photograph). Originally Episcopalian.

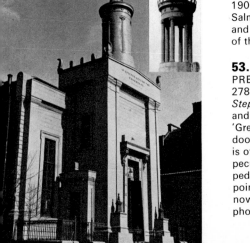

54. TRINITY DUKE STREET CHURCH, 176 Duke St. 1857. *Peddie & Kinnear*. Built as Sydney Place United Presbyterian Church—a lush Grecian was greatly favoured by the U.P. congregations at this date.

55. GLASGOW NECROPOLIS, approached from Cathedral Sq. Laid out 1833. The Bridge of Sighs, 1833, Gates, 1838, Lodge, 1839, are by the *Hamiltons;* the Jews' Enclosure, the Catacombs and Egyptian Vaults, 1836-7, by *John Bryce;* Knox's monument by *Thomas Hamilton* of Edinburgh, 1825, preceded the cemetery. Illustrated, on left, Menteith Mausoleum, 1842, by *David Cousin,* upper right, the Moorish 'Kiosk', to the traveller William Rae Wilson, by *J. A. Bell, c.* 1849; and, below, the Davidson of Ruchill Mausoleum by *J. T. Rochead,* 1851.

56

57

56. Grosvenor Terrace. 1855. *J. T. Rochead.* Like Charles Wilson, Rochead was one of David Hamilton's ex-draughtsmen. In the repetitive design of Venetian palaces he found inspiration for this terrace just as Thomson (see Nos. 66 and 71) appears to have found it in the Greek stoa. Here the theme is spectacularly stretched out with roof and chimneys all consistently on the Venetian model. KELVINSIDE PARISH CHURCH, across Byres Road at the end of the terrace, by *J. J. Stevenson,* 1862, is, appropriately, Italian Gothic.

57. Park Circus. Designed 1855. *Charles Wilson.* The Park area (with surrounding parkland laid out by *Sir Joseph Paxton*) is probably the grandest town planning enterprise in mid-Victorian Britain. The architecture, except for Park Church (No. 59), is all by Wilson (see also No. 58). Park Circus is the very hub of the area; parts to the north of it were not quite completed, or changed in execution. (It was originally intended that the new Glasgow University building be erected on this site.)

58. TRINITY COLLEGE, Lynedoch St. 1856-61. *Charles Wilson.* Originally the Free Church College. Its three Lombard towers—the tallest triumphantly evolved through several designs—combine with Rochead's Park Church (No. 59) to dominate the Park hilltop. Inside, a splendid cortile central hall. The church, left, later converted to a library and given remarkable arched concrete ceiling by *Colin Menzies,* 1909.

59. PARK CHURCH, Lynedoch Pl. 1858. *J. T. Rochead.* Impressively grand with the steep clerestory gablets and the very pointed arches. Tower provides a splendid gothic foil to Wilson's three Lombard ones (see No. 58), forming one of the finest silhouettes of modern times.

60. THE KNOWE, 301 Albert Dr., Pollokshields. *c.* 1851-3. *Alexander Thomson*. Earliest, and least known, of Thomson's larger houses. At first Thomson had a Graeco-Romanesque dual personality; he dropped Romanesque after 1856—it is said an arch of his failed. In this house his characteristic domestic formula is already evident (compare Holmwood, No. 62). His early partner and brother-in-law, John Baird II, may have had some influence on the round arch phase of his work.

61. DOUBLE VILLA, 25, 25a Mansionhouse Dr., Langside. 1856. *Alexander Thomson*. Brilliant design with reversed plans making two houses look like one; Thomson's dislike of symmetry in short elevations, rather than the aggrandizement of the separate households, is probably behind the idea. Though Thomson is unlikely to have known Ledoux's work, his low-pitched broad-eaved roofs show some similarity to it. In the ground floor bay his first experiment in separation of glazing from load-bearing structure; characteristic lotus chimney pots.

62. CONVENT OF OUR LADY OF THE MISSIONS, HOLMWOOD HOUSE, Netherlee Rd. 1856-8. *Alexander Thomson*. His greatest house, magnificently furnished within, brimming over with original ideas such as the top-lighting of the sideboard (now altar) in the dining room and the bay window of two-thirds of a circle with glazing completely free of load-bearing structure. Note how the composition builds up from left to right and how lodge, stables, garden wall and gates all form part of it.

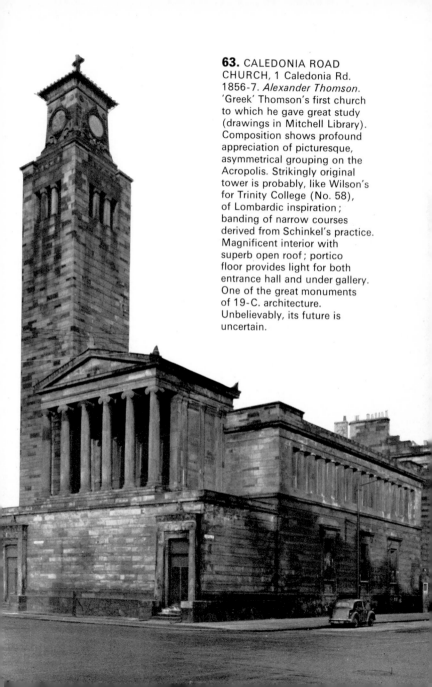

63. CALEDONIA ROAD
CHURCH, 1 Caledonia Rd.
1856-7. *Alexander Thomson.*
'Greek' Thomson's first church
to which he gave great study
(drawings in Mitchell Library).
Composition shows profound
appreciation of picturesque,
asymmetrical grouping on the
Acropolis. Strikingly original
tower is probably, like Wilson's
for Trinity College (No. 58),
of Lombardic inspiration;
banding of narrow courses
derived from Schinkel's practice.
Magnificent interior with
superb open roof; portico
floor provides light for both
entrance hall and under gallery.
One of the great monuments
of 19-C. architecture.
Unbelievably, its future is
uncertain.

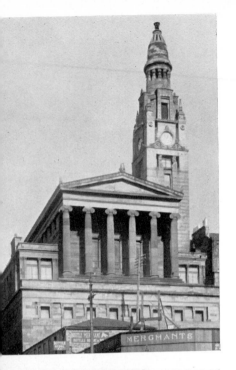

64. ST. VINCENT STREET CHURCH (SPIRITUALIST NATIONAL CHURCH), 265 St. Vincent St. 1859. *Alexander Thomson.* Built, like Caledonia Road (No. 63), as a United Presbyterian Church. Commission secured by Thomson's brother George who is said to have modified design of tower. Raised on a huge podium containing halls and other apartments. Original ideas abound, particularly the pilastrade clerestory. Impressive unorthodox tower, though most of its details have some classical precedent (despite Thomson's interest in James Fergusson's studies it is doubtful if much was really inspired by India). The peristyle columns were further developed in the Grecian buildings (see No. 67). With Caledonia Road Church and the war-destroyed Queen's Park Church takes its place among the great European churches of its age.

65. GROSVENOR BUILDING, 68-80 Gordon St. *c.* 1862. *Alexander Thomson.* A speculation of some complexity by 'Greek' Thomson and his brother George. Represents the second development of his warehouse theme with the first floor pilastrade brought in front of the giant order as aedicules. Here, for the first time, is Thomson's eaves gallery which, though possibly inspired by Schinkel, substitutes consoles for pilasters. *J. H. Craigie* used it as a pedestal for his Graeco-Baroque top hamper, 1907. At right, FORSYTH'S by *Boucher & Cousland,* 1858, later re-modelled by *Sir J. J. Burnet,* 1896-1902.

66. 1-10 Moray Place, Strathbungo. 1859. *Alexander Thomson*. Design probably suggested by the repetitive unit of the Greek stoa with which the problems of terrace design had special congruity. Thomson here introduced his characteristic incised ornament ('chip carving') which may inherit something from similar work in Thomas Hamilton's Arthur Lodge, Edinburgh.

67. GRECIAN BUILDING, 336-56 Sauchiehall St. *c*.1865. *Alexander Thomson*. Modest in scale but inventive in design. As there are only three storeys the pilastrade and the eaves gallery (see No. 65) are telescoped and, on this floor, the squat columns stand free in front of the glazing —a commercial development of experiments at Langside (No. 61) and Holmwood (No. 62). In 1865 this was quite revolutionary and reveals Thomson as one of the most original thinkers not merely in architectural style but in structure.

68. EGYPTIAN HALLS, 84-100 Union St. 1871-3. *Alexander Thomson*. Shows the penultimate step (the last, in Bath St., now destroyed) in the development of the eaves gallery which has now become a colonnade in its own right. On first and second floors there is re-working of the Gordon St. theme (No. 65) with the lower pilastrade brought further forward than the one above it and being provided with rich console capitals. The interior is iron columned. Oldfield's was the last of the original shop fronts; since this photograph the style of Jackson's has taken over.

69. Walmer Crescent. 1859-62. *Alexander Thomson.* All subtly-angled straight frontages without, in fact, one curved line. Characteristic features include the pilastrades, the banding of the masonry and the linked half-length architraves of first floor windows. Design full of subtleties warranting careful study: note how the parts between the bay windows are slightly advanced, and how the chimneys rest on solid portions of the top-floor pilastrade thus emphasizing these projections. His contemporary Queen's Park Terrace at 355-429 Eglinton Street was declared beyond repair in 1965.

70. 200 Nithsdale Road. 1868-9. *Alexander Thomson.* A rare example of a symmetrical Thomson villa, with very 'Egyptian' columns. (In general Thomson avoided symmetry in domestic design; the larger symmetrical houses of this family at Lenzie and elsewhere are the work of his last partner Robert Turnbull.)

71. 41-53 Oakfield Ave. *c.* 1865. *Alexander Thomson.* Twin pediments echo Moray Pl. (No. 66) but otherwise quite different and larger in scale. First floor has the linked quarter-length architraves, hallmark of Thomson's style at the period; square-column porches pick up the pilastrade theme of end bays.

72. Great Western Terrace. *c.* 1870. *Alexander Thomson.* The most famous of Thomson's terraces though, in fact, the simplest; relies entirely on subtle skill in the massing and detail. No. 8 contains fine interior work by *Sir Robert Lorimer* for Sir William Burrell, the great art collector.

73. ST. RONAN'S PREPARATORY SCHOOL, 202 Nithsdale Rd. *c.* 1871. *Alexander Thomson.* Unmistakably by Thomson though the attribution is without documentation. The exterior is simpler than it would have been in the 50s while the composition is a variation on old themes. The interior however is uncommonly magnificent—one of the best surviving.

74. 21-39 Hyndland Rd (formerly Westbourne Terrace). 1874. *Alexander Thomson.* The last Thomson terrace and, in design, perhaps the cleverest of them all. By 1874 the demand for bay windows could not be ignored, and seldom have they been so successfully treated. Those on the ground floor are linked together by Ionic porches to form a continuous podium supporting those on the floor above. Ironwork inimitably Thomson's.

75. St. Vincent Cres. Begun 1849.
Alexander Kirkland. Originally Stobcross
Cres. Laid out by a syndicate headed by
James Scott who had bought the land in
1844. Its long snaking line (the part not
illustrated forms a convex curve) was an
original and successful idea giving interest
to what might have been a monotonous
scheme. Square-column porches, popular in
Glasgow, derive from David Hamilton.

76. Minerva St. *c.* 1853. Part of the
Stobcross estate development begun at
Corunna St. and St. Vincent Cres. (No. 75)
with *Alexander Kirkland* as architect.
Minerva St.'s arched and pilastered corners,
of Edinburgh inspiration, are different in
character both from Kirkland's work at that
date and his neo-Venetianism of the mid-
fifties (see No. 44). Rich Corinthian capitals
and spacious layout strike an unexpected
note in this now forlorn area.

77. Crown Circus. 1859-60. *James Thomson*,
successor of the first John Baird. Earliest
part of large scheme of James Thomson
terraces and a good example of his style
before late Victorian affluence demanded
big bay windows and richer treatment, as
in his later Belhaven terraces.

78. NATIONAL COMMERCIAL BANK.
Gordon St. nr. Buchanan St. 1855. *David
Rhind*. Most of Rhind's working life was
spent building for the Commercial Bank—
from the Graeco-Roman Edinburgh head
office downwards. His most famous design
is the Venetian-style Edinburgh Life
Association in Edinburgh but this, according
to a Ferrarese pattern, is equally good. First
floor very characteristic. Sculpture by Alex
Handyside Ritchie.

79. CHRISTIAN SCIENCE CHURCH
(formerly QUEEN'S ROOMS), 1 La Belle
Pl. 1857. *Charles Wilson*. In its magnificent
rhythm and sophisticated personal handling
of early Italian themes this is the epitome
of Wilson's style. In their small scale detail
and rather broken design the adjacent
houses, designed by Wilson in the same
year, cleverly accentuate the bigness of his
concept.

78

79

80. ROYAL FACULTY OF PROCURATORS, 62 and 68 West George St. 1854. *Charles Wilson*. Designed in record time after a previous scheme by Emmett of London was abandoned. The smallest but most richly finished example of the Venetian phase in Glasgow architecture. Remarkable for the brilliant interiors contrived within its small space, particularly the long, very grand, Genoese staircase. The lawlord keystones on the exterior carved by A. H. Ritchie.

81. BANK OF SCOTLAND, St. Vincent Pl. and George Sq. 1869. *J. T. Rochead*. Rochead's last works were of an exceptionally high academic order. Here the design has all the energy of his early work without any of the bizarre elements. The elevation to George Sq. was shortly after made part of a grand near-symmetrical composition with the Bank Buildings by *Sellars* 1874, and Merchants' House by *Burnet*. Sculptor of the great atlantes, William Mossman. The urns in the photograph now removed.

82. Former STIRLING'S LIBRARY, 46-56 Miller St. 1863-5. *James Smith*. Smith died in the latter part of 1863 and the building was completed by Melvin and Leiper. Smith's largest building is Treron's in Sauchiehall St. His later years were clouded by his daughter Madeleine's murder trial.

83. JOHN STREET CHURCH, 18 John St 1859-60. *J. T. Rochead*. Typical of Rochead's mid-career Mannerist style; the directly glazed colonnades are a strikingly original feature though doubtless having their origin in Thomson's experiments in fenestration.

84. Former YATE STREET POLICE STATION, 976 Gallowgate. *c.* 1877. *John Carrick*. A neat minor piece of civic architecture with a portico whose only purpose seems to be to give interest to a dismal area; it almost reminds one of Ledoux's Paris *Barrières*. Carrick, city architect-planner-engineer during the period of greatest expansion, was a solid, though somewhat conservative designer.

85

86

87. Former STOW COLLEGE,
119-25 Cowcaddens St. 1846.
Thomas Burns. Built as the Free
Normal Seminary in elegant, still
rather Georgian, Gothic. Later
additions by Campbell Douglas
and Stevenson. Although Burns
practised in Glasgow no other work
by him within the city is at present
known.

85. LANDSDOWNE CHURCH, Gt. Western Rd. at Kelvin Br. 1863. *John Honeyman*. An early work by the first Glasgow architect to achieve a high academic standard in Gothic; the fine Early English detail by John Mossman. Its graceful slender spire, with that of St. Mary's (No. 86), punctuates Gt. Western Rd.'s unbroken vista. Interior, a period piece of great interest: aisles are corridors with an individual door to each pew in Gothic version of typical galleried auditorium favoured by United Presbyterians—a long way from the simplicity of the early Secession kirks.

86. ST. MARY'S EPISCOPAL CATHEDRAL, Gt. Western Rd. and Holyrood Cres. 1871-84; spire completed 1893. *Sir George Gilbert Scott*, completed by his son *John Oldrid Scott*. Pure academic Early English verging on Early Decorated with no personal Scott inventions, as in University (No. 88), and better for their absence. Interior attractive with open timber roofs: wagon-kingpost in chancel, and wooden groin vault at crossing.

88. GLASGOW UNIVERSITY, Gilmorehill. Completed 1870. *Sir George Gilbert Scott*. It was (and still is to be) regretted that one of the first rate Glasgow architects was not given the commission, but Scott's building (A), a notable Glasgow landmark, is not as bad as it is sometimes made out to be; it should, moreover, be remembered that the layout (Baird, 1846) was specified beforehand. *John Oldrid Scott*, who added the Bute Hall (B) and its undercroft (C), wisely thought out something different for the spire. Scott tells us that its stylistic trial run was the Albert Institute in Dundee.

88

A

B

C

89. ST. ANDREW'S HALLS, Granville St. (and Berkeley St. and Kent Rd.). 1873-7. *James Sellars*. Cunningham of Liverpool was called in to advise but the job was taken over at sketch plan stage by Sellars, then only 30. The design, in the Schinkel-Thomson manner he favoured, must have been entirely his own. It is extraordinary that such a young architect at such a late date should accept what, elsewhere, had become an outmoded fashion; but, in Glasgow, Thomson had proved to his contemporaries that neo-Greek was still a living style. The huge sculpture groups are by John Mossman. Gutted by fire it awaits a decision on its future.

90. KELVINSIDE ACADEMY,
Bellshaugh Rd. 1877-9. *James
Sellars*. Though never a pupil of
Thomson, Sellars here comes
closest to his style: the pilastrades,
the chimneys and the glazing are
all pure Thomson. But Sellars was
always careful to avoid
Thomsonesque inventions that
were 'not in the book'; nor does
he devise new ones of his own.
In consequence, he never quite
matches Thomson's brilliance and
profundity.

91

91. KELVINGROVE PARISH
CHURCH, Derby St. and Bentinck
St. 1878-80. *James Sellars*. Built
as Finnieston Church; one of
Sellars's last pure Greek designs
(it might almost be 1818-20).
The banding on the lower portion
and the screens in the peristyle
are features of Thomson
derivation; the filled-in pediment
reduces the number of pigeon
perching places.

92

92. CORNHILL HOUSE,
144-6 West George St. 1879-81.
James Sellars. Formerly the New
Club, a breakaway now re-united
with the Western Club. By late
1878 Sellars seems to have come
to the conclusion that to
persevere with the Greek revival
was flying in the face of history,
and perhaps financially
inexpedient. In this transitional
building a modified French, with
much low relief sculpture, was
adopted. Thomson's influence is,
however, still present in the third-
floor-window pilastrades.

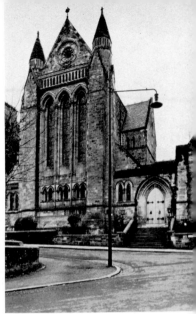

93. BELMONT AND HILLHEAD PARISH CHURCH, Huntly Gdns. 1875-6. *James Sellars*. The Sainte-Chapelle theme is rare in Presbyterian church-building, particularly on a scale such as this. Interior groin vaulted in wood. Winner of a limited competition in which Leiper and Honeyman also took part; though it was Sellars who won, the general scheme (according to the late W. H. McNab) was Leiper's. Much preliminary discussion is said to have taken place with a view to eliminating all columns. Good angel sculpture on exterior; glass includes some by Burne-Jones.

96. BELHAVEN-WESTBOURNE CHURCH, 52 Westbourne Gdns. 1880. *John Honeyman*. Handsome example of Honeyman's Italian Renaissance manner for a wealthy west end Free Church congregation. Large galleried interior similar to that of Barony North (No. 97).

94. ST. LUKE'S GREEK ORTHODOX CHURCH, 29 Dundonald Rd. 1877. *James Sellars*. Formerly Belhaven Church. Sellars's best gothic design—a striking example of his versatility and talent before his powers were blunted by overwork in the eighties. Perhaps, too, an example of his persuasiveness; for here he built for a United Presybyterian congregation what in structure, if not furnishings, was distinctly Episcopalian.

95. Former BARONY FREE CHURCH, 49-53 Castle St. 1866-7. *John Honeyman*. The oldest, after the Cathedral, of the remarkable group of churches round Cathedral Sq. The Franco-Scots saddleback tower is an attractive feature in the neighbourhood of the Cathedral, but the church itself is badly deteriorated. By the same architect as the very different Barony North (No. 97).

95

97. BARONY NORTH CHURCH, 18-20 Cathedral Sq. 1878. *John Honeyman*. Good example of Honeyman's Italianate manner with well-designed tower. Interior large and galleried—very United Presbyterian compared with the Roman exuberance of the exterior.

98. STOCK EXCHANGE, Buchanan St. and St. Georges Pl. 1875-7.
John Burnet, Sr. Gothic was rarely employed in Glasgow for secular
buildings; this is Burnet's only essay in medieval Franco-Venetian.
Sir J. J. Burnet, in his skilful addition (right), alleviated the original heftiness.
An important constituent of this very rich stretch of Buchanan St.

99. COURTHOUSES (formerly LANARKSHIRE HOUSE and before that
UNION BANK), 191 Ingram St. 1876-9. *John Burnet.* Originally a
mansion; David Hamilton rebuilt it as a bank with a tall classical
portico in 1841. Present façade, with sculpture by John Mossman, built to
gain space and owes something to late Cockerell as well as to Venice.
Hamilton's columns from the portico were re-used by Campell Douglas
at the Citizen's Theatre. (*top right*)

100. CLYDESDALE BANK,
30 St. Vincent Pl. 1870-3.
John Burnet. The part on the left
was added subsequently though
doubtless intended from the first;
symmetry, however, was not
achieved as the 'Citizen' newspaper
beat the Bank at the other end
to the eastern part of the intended
site. At the time there was unkind
comment about Burnet's departure
from his normal Wilsonesque
Italian; today it seems engagingly
expensive and exuberant.

101. Cleveden Crescent. *c.* 1876. *John Burnet.* One of the most elegant of Glasgow's west end terraces. The single storey bay windows have affinities with the younger Burnet's work and indeed, in the reduced scale and absence of basement areas, the characteristic Edwardian Glasgow terrace may be said to have been pioneered.

102. Former FINE ART INSTITUTE, 171 Sauchiehall St. 1879-80. *Sir J. J. Burnet.* The younger Burnet's first design after his return from the Atelier Pascal in the Ecole des Beaux-Arts. Exquisitely detailed neo-Greek is as Glaswegian as Parisian, but French schooling was plain in the fine central doorway, now destroyed. Frieze by John Mossman. The building on the right was designed by *John Keppie,* Honeyman's partner, in 1896.

103. COLLEGE OF DRAMATIC ART, St. George's Pl. 1886. *Sir J. J. Burnet.* Originally the Athenaeum. Such clean simplicity was something new in British architecture of the 1880s. Effective use of sculpture groups reminiscent of St. Andrews Halls (No. 84) ; the four standing figures, and probably the groups, by John Mossman. The familiar Burnet architrave and other characteristic features make an early appearance.

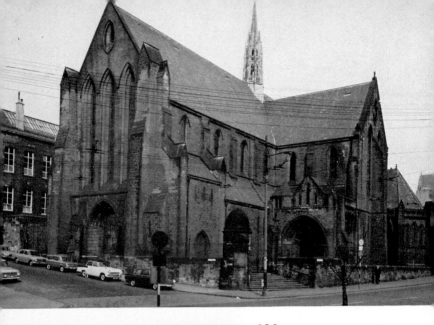

104. BARONY CHURCH,
1 Castle St. by Cathedral Sq.
1886-90. *Sir J. J. Burnet* and
John A. Campbell. Winner in a
competition, the assessor being
J. L. Pearson to whose known
preferences for Early Pointed and
the Gerona scheme of nave
Burnet and Campbell's design
was shrewdly directed. Front
based on Dunblane Cathedral.
Nave and chancel (B) in Gerona
arrangement. Not only the church
but the halls and subsidiary rooms
designed with exceptional
fastidiousness. Burnet or
Campbell? It is hard to say:
Burnet usually gets the credit,
but Campbell's Shawlands Old,
1888, is very close in style. The
cost was long unkindly remembered,
particularly by some of the
unsuccessful competitors.

B

105. CLYDE TRUST BUILDING, 16 Robertson St. 1883-6 and 1905-8. *Sir J. J. Burnet.* Beaux-Arts Renaissance indeed —but with hints of Sellars also. A campanile was at one time contemplated for the Broomielaw corner but a dome with sculpture by Albert Hodge, was finally decided on.

106. QUEEN MARGARET UNION, University Ave. 1887 and 1895. *Sir J. J. Burnet* of Burnet, Son & Campbell. At present housing the Glasgow University women students' union. English collegiate Gothic but with a squat, rather Scottish, tower; absence of any crowning feature points forward to Mackintosh and the kind of Gothic revival work done in the first third of this century. The Botany Building, completed 1901, a little further down University Ave. is by the same architect in conjunction with *Oldrid Scott.* (*centre*)

107. CHARING CROSS MANSIONS, Sauchiehall St. and St George's Rd. 1891. *Sir J. J. Burnet.* Parisian schooling comes out strongly in this spectacular corner with *grande horloge* (now handless and neglected) surrounded by sympathetically related sculpture. The eaves gallery, a Thomson feature greatly favoured by Burnet, here makes a first appearance. The infill is in glazed tile. The shop fronts are not notable for their harmony.

108. WELLINGTON CHURCH University Ave. 1883. *T. L. Watson.* One would not think from this Presbyterian version of the Madeleine that Watson had been trained under Alfred Waterhouse. He was not a brilliant architect but here he rose to the occasion magnificently. Interior galleried with a fine ceiling.

109. ST. GEORGE'S-IN-THE-FIELDS, 485 St. George's Rd. 1886. *Hugh* and *David Barclay* probably Hugh who was much the better designer and a close friend of his ex-pupil Sellars. The last great work of *ancien régime* classicism; pediment with sculpture by Birnie Rhind makes the portico one of the very finest in Glasgow.

110. LANGSIDE HILL CHURCH, 122 Langside Ave. 1895-6. *Alexander Skirving.* A very late church in the Thomson vein by his one time chief draughtsman; but by 1895-6 memories of his master's voice were growing faint. At left Battlefield Monument, 1887 also by Skirving; his Langside Old Church nearby demonstrates inferiority of Gothic to Greek— at least in his personal practice

111. CITY CHAMBERS, George Sq. 1883-8. *William Young*. A London Scot, he was awarded the commission after two competitions. The designs were published and show that most competitors found the height to width proportions and a satisfactory relationship between building and tower difficult, and, notwithstanding its faults, Young's win was not altogether undeserved. Interior (B), especially staircase, of staggering magnificence with very rich use of materials. Sculptor, George Lawson.

B

112. Former ANDERSON'S COLLEGE OF MEDICINE, 56 Dumbarton Rd. 1888-9. *James Sellars*. His last building, completed by his draughtsman, *John Keppie*. Sellars's Renaissance style of the 1880s was not always attractive but here, inspired perhaps by Rowand Anderson, it is pleasing and successful. Sculpture by Pittendrigh Macgillivray.

113. CENTRAL STATION HOTEL,
Gordon St. and Hope St. 1884. *Sir Rowand Anderson*. In the late 1870s the Caledonian Railway crossed the river and bought their way into the heart of the city at fantastic cost. The hotel was an impressive monument to their arrival. Anderson, an Edinburgh architect, is often regarded as the Scottish Norman Shaw; not a great innovator he practised in many styles all at a very high academic level.

114. TEMPLETON'S CARPET FACTORY,
by Glasgow Green. 1889. *William Leiper*. Brilliant piece of Victorian advertising in polychrome brick and tile with stone dressings. Antipathy towards the architect from the engineer brought about a fatal collapse during construction. Leiper was a shy retiring batchelor; when the City Bank

crash brought Depression conditions to Glasgow he went to study painting at Julien's Academy in Paris, though he was back as soon as financial prosperity returned.

115. 118 Tradeston Street. *c.* 1890.
William F. McGibbon. An inexpensive version of the Templeton theme (see No. 114) in Bargello gothic—successful and amusing attempt to make an ordinary brick warehouse look interesting. The crude repair to the lower crenellation is all too typical—surely I.C.I., with all its resources, could do better than this. McGibbon an interesting minor architect; his best work, the Corn Exchange, has lately been destroyed.

116. CLYDESDALE BANK, 91 Buchanan St. 1896. *Sir George Washington Browne.* Designed as a tearoom by an Edinburgh architect famed for bank architecture it subsequently caught the Clydesdale's eye. Exquisitely detailed François Ier to the requirements of Miss Kate Cranston's fastidious taste; it once contained furniture and fittings by George Walton and a startlingly original mural by C. R. Mackintosh.

117. PEARCE INSTITUTE, 840 Govan Rd. 1903 and 1905. *Sir Rowand Anderson* of Edinburgh. The shipbuilders were generous to Govan and chose their architects with discernment (Elder employed Burnet; Pearce, Rowand Anderson). Their buildings redeem a bleak area. At this date Anderson favoured the Scots 17-C. Renaissance style

both early and late. This, an example of the former, is handled with scholarship and skill. The nearby Govan Old Parish Church, 1884, is also by Anderson.

118. SCOTTISH CO-OPERATIVE WHOLESALE SOCIETY, 95 Morrison St. Completed 1897. *Bruce & Hay.* A warehouse in scale and elaboration to eclipse all others and to boost the rising prestige of the co-operative movement. The building evokes wonder rather than pleasure; it was said that the architects had re-used their Municipal Buildings competition design, but this they hotly denied. The adjacent No. 71 by *James Ferrigan*, 1919-33, is (less dome) almost equally grand and has more positive merits.

119. DOULTON FOUNTAIN, Glasgow Green. 1888. Surely the most astonishing piece of earthenware ever made. Devised by A. E. Pearce of Messrs. Doulton for the Exhibition of 1888, Victoria presides over her peoples. It was presented to the City and re-erected in the Green in 1890. A fascinating object once one's first instinctive dislike of the colour is overcome.

120. WOOLWICH EQUITABLE BUILDING, 106-8 Hope St. 1894. *William Forrest Salmon* perhaps assisted by his son *James Salmon II*. Art Nouveau is still a year or two away. Salmon was for a time with Sir G. G. Scott. The buildings to the rear in Renfield Lane are by Mackintosh.

121. Former SUN LIFE BUILDING, 117-121 West George St. and 38-42 Renfield St. 1889-1893. *William Leiper*. François Ier on a grand commercial scale; the French were sufficiently impressed to give it a silver medal at the 1900 Paris Exhibition. The sculpture is by Birnie Rhind; W. J. Anderson is said to have drawn the details.

120

121

22. CAMPHILL-QUEEN'S PARK CHURCH, Balvicar St. 1878, spire 1883. *William Leiper*. His best church within the city, more confidently handled than his earlier tall-spired church at Dowanhill, 1865-6, which is charged with admiration for Burges in some of the details, though the general outline is, as here, Normandy Gothic—as might be expected from a pupil of J. L. Pearson.

23. ST. NINIAN'S WYND CHURCH, Cathcart Rd. and Crown St. 1888. *W. G. Rowan*. At first a Thomson follower (his is the large church on Shields Rd., Pollokshields, of 1875) Rowan soon became a skilful practitioner in the Gothic and Romanesque. This church is probably his best and in its rich and highly successful treatment of the Romanesque theme shows the influence of the work of H. H. Richardson of Boston. Rowan's church at Strathbungo, done two years earlier, is an amusing amalgam of Romanesque and late Gothic.

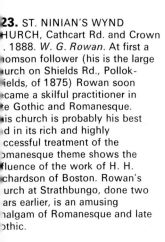

124

125

126

124. WATERLOO CHAMBERS,
15-23 Waterloo St. 1899. *Sir J. J. Burnet*. Complex design originally intended to be higher.

125. ATLANTIC CHAMBERS,
43-7 Hope St. 1899. *Sir J. J. Burnet*. Bold design of seven storeys, very forward looking in its simplicity; an effective eaves gallery.

126. ROYAL SCOTTISH ACADEMY OF MUSIC: ATHENAEUM,
179 Buchanan St. 1891-3. *J. J. Burnet* and *J. A. Campbell*. The pioneer narrow frontage vertical composition in Glasgow. Narrow frontages were to be a common feature in Glasgow as the Georgian house plots were redeveloped and the arch and bay window motif formed the basis of many subsequent designs. Generally credited to Burnet, but closer to Campbell's later work.

127. SAVINGS BANK OF GLASGOW,
177 Ingram St. 1866 and 1896-1900. *John Burnet Sr.* and *Sir J. J. Burnet*. The original 3-storey building fronts Glassford St.; to this Burnet, the son, added a colonnaded top floor and a splendid single-storey banking hall in which his baroque manner achieved maturity. Sculpture by Sir George Frampton.

128. McGEOCH'S, 28 West Campbell Street. 1905. *Sir J. J. Burnet*. The vertical integration of fenestration at 2nd, 3rd and 4th floors is final outcome of many Glasgow experiments going back to Thomson's Dunlop Street design of 1849 (No. 40); mullioned treatment may owe something to Louis Sullivan but probably arrived at independently. Sculpture by Phyllis Archibald. Progenitor of Kodak House, London (1911) and though less 'modern' its modelling is bolder. Probably Burnet's masterpiece.

127

128

129. ELDER LIBRARY, 228a Langlands Rd. 1902-3. *Sir J. J. Burnet*. Mature Burnet baroque. Curve of portico no doubt of Austrian inspiration; detail, however, is typical Burnet particularly the widely spaced balusters. The building extended later. (*above*)

130. ELDER COTTAGE HOSPITAL, Drumoyne Rd. 1902-3. *Sir J. J. Burnet*. 'Wrenaissance' of exceptional academic fidelity. Low lines with big broad-eaved roof and pretty Carolean details strike a homely domestic note in contrast to most hospital building of the period. Nurses' home opposite is also by Burnet but unrelated in design. (*centre*)

131. SCOTTISH PROVIDENT INSTITUTION, 17-29 St. Vincent Pl. 1906. *J. M. Dick Peddie*. His largest building. Ever-increasing demands for size and height in commercial buildings was now taxing the ingenuity of the academic school. Here Peddie adopted a French Renaissance style, probably for its roof capacity. Elegant porch over basement adds a luxurious note. (*left*)

132. PARCELS OFFICE, 48, 36
Waterloo St. *c*. 1906. *W. T. Oldreive*.
Like Government architecture at this date
it is inevitably academic ; but of a heroic
scale and a high standard ; the great
'thermae' windows very successful.
(*above*)

133. NATIONAL COMMERCIAL BANK,
St. Vincent St. and Buchanan St. 1900.
J. M. Dick Peddie, one of the few
Edinburgh contemporaries of Rowand
Anderson to approach his quality.
Edwardian skyline flourishes were foreign
to his nature but there is often a kind of
baroque restlessness in the details.
(*centre*)

134. ROYAL SCOTTISH ACADEMY
OF MUSIC, St. George's Pl. and
Buchanan St. 1909. *A. N. Paterson*.
Built as the Liberal Club ; red Dumfries-
shire stone. A more richly modelled
building than his St. Enoch Sq. bank
(see No. 166). The balcony, at right, is
neatly linked with that of Burnet's
Athenaeum (No. 126). (*right*)

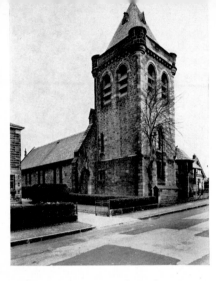

135. BROOMHILL CONGREGATIONAL CHURCH, Victoria Park Gdns. South. *c.* 1900. *Sir J. J. Burnet.* Typical later Burnet church: low and friendly rather than aspiring. Squat tower with pyramid roof. Its kin are churches at Larbert and Brechin. At St. Margaret's Tollcross (No. 140) Rowan was thinking on rather similar lines.

136. STEVENSON MEMORIAL CHURCH Belmont St. at Belmont Bridge. Designed 1898, built 1900-2. *J. J. Stevenson* of London. Crown steeple; very finely detailed work inside and out. Stevenson had been a partner of Campbell Douglas and is chiefly remembered for the Italian gothic church at Kelvinside (see No. 56) In his later years he designed a number c Scots Gothic Free Churches of which this is perhaps the finest. In his work in the South he was a tasteful exponent of the 'Queen Anne' style.

137. ST. JAMES' PARISH CHURCH, Meiklerig Cres. Pollok. 1893 as Titwood Parish Church by *H. E. Clifford*; re-erected on present site by *Thomson, McCrea & Sanders,* 1953-4. Clifford's style owes something to Burnet but here the late Gothic motifs are typically his own. (A good smaller church by the same architect is Carntyne-St. Michael's on Edrom St.) The transportation of this church suggests a possible method for saving some of the better city churches now threatened.

138. ST. BRIDE'S EPISCOPAL CHURCH, Hyndland Rd. and Kingsborough Gdns. Interior, 1904, by G. F. *Bodley* of London; other work, 1915, *H. O. Tarbolton* of Edinburgh. Unfortunately unfinished with an aisle and a porch unbuilt. Chancel is Bodley's; nave was reconstructed and west end built by Tarbolton. A fine example of the scholarly and tasteful final phase of the Gothic Revival by two of its most skilful practitioners.

139. ST. MARGARET'S EPISCOPAL CHURCH, 351 Kilmarnock Rd. 1912. *Dr. P. Macgregor Chalmers.* Chalmers made his name with a simple, distinctive Scots Romanesque. His most important early work is not in Glasgow though there is a series of smaller churches notable for good interior work. St. Margaret's is a German 'double-ender'. The tower was completed by *White & Galloway* after the First World War.

140. ST. MARGARET'S TOLLCROSS CHURCH, 179 Braidfauld St. 1900-1. *J. G. Rowan.* An English village church for Glasgow's east end. Rowan, when circumstances permitted, was an exquisite artist in miniature: it is a matter for regret that, after his early Thomson-esque church at Pollokshields, he had no big opportunities.

141. GLASGOW HERALD
BUILDING : MITCHELL
STREET EXTENSION. 1893-5.
John Keppie with *Charles
Rennie Mackintosh* assisting.
Main lines by Keppie but the
tower and a good deal else
drawn by Mackintosh. Both
the Keppie and the Mackintosh
elements were singularly
advanced for 1893. What
prompted the design of the
top of the tower? It is hard
indeed to say.

142. ST. CUTHBERT'S AND
QUEEN'S CROSS CHURCH,
866 Garscube Rd. 1897-99.
C. R. Mackintosh of Honeyman
& Keppie. Honeyman had a
large church building practice
and was able to entrust this
commission to Mackintosh. Art
Nouveau Gothic of a very
original variety; tower, however,
developed from a medieval
one which caught Mackintosh's
eye at Merriot, Somerset. Note
the reverse curve of the arches
and the bold convex mouldings.

143. RUCHILL CHURCH HALL, 24 Ruchill St. 1899. *C. R. Mackintosh*, of Honeyman & Keppie. A minor work, ingeniously planned. Art Nouveau had a brief fashion in churches. Just as with Salmon at St. Andrew's East (No. 144), another architect of more orthodox tastes was commissioned in 1905 to build the church—in this case Neil C. Duff whose work is decent but without originality.

144. ST. ANDREW'S EAST CHURCH HALL, 685 Alexandra Parade. 1899. *James Salmon II.* Art Nouveau Gothic with effective use of sculpture characterizes Salmon's work. He lost the commission for the church to Miller (see No. 145) and we do not know what he had in mind.

145. ST. ANDREW'S EAST CHURCH, 681 Alexandra Parade. 1904. *James Miller.* Salmon had previously designed the Hall (No. 144) but it was Miller who got the commission for the church. Though the loss of a major Salmon church is to be lamented, Miller's building is designed with originality and assurance. Other contemporary Miller churches, of rather less individuality, are Jordanhill and the Macgregor Memorial at Govan.

146A

B

C

146. GLASGOW SCHOOL OF ART, 167 Renfrew St. 1897-9 and 1907-9. *C. R. Mackintosh*, then with Honeyman & Keppie. In 1896 the Governors of the School had £21,000 for a new building, and the School's Head, Fra. Newbery, had prepared an exacting schedule of accommodation. Following a competition in which most of Glasgow's leading architects took part Mackintosh's design, the most economical and the nearest to meeting Newbery's requirements, was chosen. Though this was for the whole building, there was at the time only enough money for the part of it stretching from the east façade (C) to the main entrance (B). Ten years later the Renfrew St. façade (A) and a wholly re-designed library block (D) were completed; additions were also made to the east wing. The finished building is the most famous in Glasgow and, of its period, one of the most famous in the world. What was the nature of Mackintosh's genius? Is he to be numbered among the outstanding brilliantly accomplished exponents of the Art Nouveau? Or was he the pioneer of the Modern Movement? Was he, as he himself sometimes implied, the traditionalist drawing inspiration from many sources, not least the Scottish vernacular architecture of the 16th and 17th centuries— 'the only style we can claim as being in whole or part our own'? Or was he the prophet of functionalism? The illustrations on the two following pages (E-H from parts of the 1897-9 building; I-L from the later additions) may, in different ways, suggest affirmative answers to all these questions.

D

E

F

146. GLASGOW SCHOOL OF ART,
      1897-9 BUILDING
E *Timber trusses, Museum roof*
F *Museum and main staircase*
G *Wrought iron finial on east gable*
H *Wrought iron brackets on north
   façade*

K

L

146. GLASGOW SCHOOL OF ART,
   1907-9 ADDITIONS
I   *The Loggia and the 'Hen-run'*
J   *East staircase at first floor level*
K   *The Library: gallery*
L   *The Library: general view*

A

B

147. Former WILLOW TEAROOMS now part of DALY'S, 199 Sauchiehall St. 1904. *C. R. Mackintosh*. Though this, the last and most elaborate of Mackintosh's tearooms, is now used for other purposes it is included here because, if circumstances allowed, it could virtually be brought back to its original state. It was the only one of Miss Kate Cranston's tearooms for which Mackintosh was entirely responsible, both outside and in. Today the street front (B) has lost its ground floor and the dining room (A; here seen through the wrought metal stair balustrade) is without its furniture and fittings. Enough, however, remains—including the extraordinary plaster frieze (seen in A) and the leaded mirror door of the room de luxe—to suggest, albeit faintly, one of the most original decorative schemes of its age.

148. Former INGRAM STREET
TEAROOMS, now ZEDERBAUM'S
FANCY GOODS SHOP, 211
Ingram St. 1901-1912.
C. R. Mackintosh. One of
Mackintosh's two major tearooms
for Miss Cranston. Unlike the
Willow (No. 147) entirely a
remodelling, done over a period of
years, of existing interiors. An old
photograph of a 1901 room; the
present arrangement and the
Mackintosh tartan carpets are not
quite what the designer intended.
Bought in 1950, with all its
furniture, by the Corporation who,
it is hoped, will ensure that it is
restored in situ or elswhere.

150. SCOTLAND STREET
SCHOOL, 225 Scotland St. 1904.
C. R. Mackintosh of Honeyman,
Keppie & Mackintosh. Plan a
fairly standard one for school
buildings of that date but treatment
and details of exceptional
originality. The staircases translate
into the language of modern
architecture the form of a
'Scotch Baronial' stair tower.
In centre of façade, not visible in
illustration, a delightfully diminutive
entrance for infants. (*below*)

149. Formerly 78 Southpark Avenue. 1906.
C. R. Mackintosh. In 1906 Mackintosh and
his wife moved to a westend terrace house.
In a remodelling of the interior he used
many of the fittings from his Mains St. flat
of 1901. Now demolished; but an exact
reconstruction of the interior is to form part
of the new University Art Gallery (No. 218).

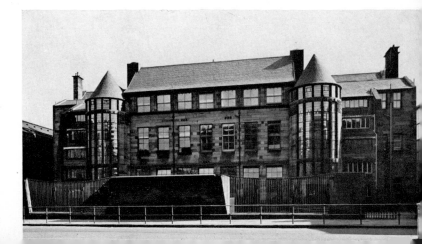

151

152

153
A & B

151. 7-23 Kirklee Rd. 1900. *John A. Campbell.* The best Glasgow example of Campbell's domestic work. Over and above its architectural merits it is interesting for the move away from the formalism and tall proportions of a generation earlier. Composite photograph showing the quite different treatment of each end block. (*left*)

152. 157-167 Hope St. and 169-175 West George St. 1902. *John A. Campbell.* This mighty commercial alcazar was perhaps inspired by A. N. Prentice's publication of his Spanish studies. Campbell's masterpiece; his later works are often more modern and powerfully designed, but none has the same romantic appeal. (*left*)

154

154. 122-8 St. Vincent St. 1904. *John A. Campbell.* A fine example of his style. Skilful in design but without either the modern fenestration of Burnet's McGeoch's (No. 128) or the simplified lines of his own 84-94 in the same street (No. 153). Steel framed but front wall still load-bearing above ground floor.

155. WESTERN TELEPHONE EXCHANGE, 24 Highburgh Rd. 1907. *Leonard Stokes* of London. A characteristically clever design by this English master of the Modern Movement; treated in very shallow relief with discreet use of polychromy in stonework. (Among Glasgow architects only Leiper and Forrest Salmon ever made much use of polychromy.)

153. 84-94 St. Vincent St. 1908. *John A. Campbell.* His last office block built in the year of his death. The fenestration of the street façade (A) is quite conventional but the soaring lines are unmistakably of the 20-C. The rear elevation (B), elaborately modelled with bay windows, strikes a modern note and is a clever anticipation of much architecture of the inter-war period. (*left*)

155

156
157

156. MERCANTILE CHAMBERS, 39-69 Bothwell St. 1898-1900. *James Salmon II*. Modern movement with details of Renaissance inspiration—a kind of *fin-de-siècle* Beardsley feeling pervades. Sculpture by Derwent Wood.

157. BRITISH LINEN BANK 816-818 Govan Rd. 1899. *James Salmon II*. Relatively orthodox in fenestration, but very Art Nouveau at main door sculpture and in the open crown top.

158. 142A-144 St. Vincent St. 1899-1902. *James Salmon II*. Ten storeys on a single house plot 29 ft. 6 in. wide but 109 ft. deep. Compositional idea based on three interlocked bays to give maximum glazed area. In consequence the stonework is whittled away to almost nothing. Art Nouveau style is peculiarly suitable for this.

159. ANDERSTON SAVINGS BANK, 752-6 Argyle St. 1899-1900. *James Salmon II*. Salmon's Art Nouveau is moving to its final form. The mosaic tympanum to the doorway is an especially fine feature and it is to be hoped it will be rescued when the building is demolished in the Anderston re-development. Sculpture by Albert Hodge.

160. LION CHAMBERS, 170-2 Hope St. 1905. *James Salmon II* and *J. Gaff Gillespie*. Early example of reinforced concrete on the Hennebique system; walls and floors only 4 in. thick though building rises 90 ft. from pavement. Site only 46 x 33 ft. ! General design with arch and bay-window motif derives from Campbell's Britannia Building in Buchanan St. which, in turn, was inspired by the Athenaeum (No. 126).

161. 12, 14 University Gdns. *c.* 1900. *J. Gaff Gillespie*. Gillespie was James Salmon II's junior partner and, as Salmon's reputation has been eclipsed by Mackintosh, Gillespie's memory has been at a double disadvantage. These buildings, especially No. 12 (on right), show him as a skilful practitioner of the Modern Movement. The lower numbers in the terrace are by *Sir J. J. Burnet,* 1896.

158

159

160

161

162. NAPIER HOUSE, 640-6 Govan Rd. 1898-9.
William James Anderson. Had he lived, this scholarly
architect would have been remembered with Mackintosh
and Salmon as a pioneer of the Modern Movement. The
strange fenestration is, perhaps, of Thomson inspiration.
Concrete, without designed reinforcement in the modern
sense, was used here; and, in 1895, he had built an
all-concrete building in McPhater St. Fourth floor addition
at right a later indiscretion.

163. 118 Howard St. *c.* 1904. *J. Gibb Morton.* The best
Glasgow example of Art Nouveau architecture outwith
the orbits of Mackintosh and Salmon; the motifs,
however, largely of Burnet and Campbell inspiration.

166. BENEFFREY, 124 Springkell Ave. 1914. *W. Hunter McNab.* No really worthy example of William Leiper's domestic buildings (so abundant in Helensburgh) survives in Glasgow; they were supplied in two styles, Franco-Scottish and Norman Shaw. This finely finished house, by his partner and successor, is a late example of the former—very much the kind of thing a rich American connoisseur of the period would have favoured. Now a University of Strathclyde women students' residence.

167. ST. ENOCH UNDERGROUND STATION, St. Enoch Square. 1896. *James Miller.* A pretty Jacobean toy-like building among towering façades of the 1870s onwards. Note the fine gable sculpture. The trains once moved by gripping a moving cable. At left in background National Commercial Bank by *A. N. Paterson*, 1906.

164. THE ROOST, 59 Dumbarton Rd. *c.* 1895-1905. Art Nouveau in Glasgow is especially associated with tearooms; there are, however, several pubs in related, if somewhat more eye-catching, style. Most, including the King's Arms in Bath St., are being 'improved' out of existence; even The Roost has lost its rustic lettering and its virtuoso artificial graining. (*left*)

165. 8-10 Lowther Terrace. *c.* 1904. *A. G. Sydney Mitchell* of Edinburgh and *James Miller.* The centre house is by Mitchell, an architect of the Rowand Anderson school who had occasional flashes of real brilliance. The other two are Miller's. An interesting experiment in terrace architecture, being unified only by scale. The other end of the terrace was not built and a dismal post-war block now occupies its site. (*left*)

168. ROYSTON SECONDARY SCHOOL, 102 Royston Rd. 1906. *Duncan McNaughtan* and *Alan G. McNaughtan.* A good example of the influence of Mackintosh on contemporary architecture and the only school of its period to compare with Scotland Street (No. 150): though not so bold in design it is handled with sensitivity. Any view of it is unhappily obscured by extraneous outhouses.

169. CITY CHAMBERS EXTENSION, Cochrane St. 1923. *Watson, Salmond & Gray.* The result of a 2-tier open competition in 1913. Shows admiration for style of François Mansart who was the hero of Reginald Blomfield's hypercritical history of French Renaissance, 1911. Connected to Young's building (No. 111) across John St. by outstandingly fine pair of arches (*above left*).

170. PHOENIX ASSURANCE BUILDING, 78 St. Vincent St. 1913. *A. D. Hislop.* The prototype of the commercial buildings of the inter-war years and the first in which building high in classic style was satisfactorily solved. Edwardian exuberance is out: a monumental neo-classicism is in.

171. BANK OF SCOTLAND,
110-120 St. Vincent St. 1927. *James Miller*. A development of Hislop's Phoenix design (No. 170) of 1913 which formed the basis of many inter-war designs. Greek detail supersedes the Baroque of Miller's pre-1914 designs. In his later years Miller was assisted by Richard Gunn, a very clever designer.

172. 200 St. Vincent St. *c.* 1929. *Burnet, Son & Dick* largely by Sir J. J. Burnet himself and virtually his last design. Treatment is masterly though, unlike McGeoch's (No. 128), there are no great innovations in fenestration. Here shown just after completion; later, some sculpture was added to the façade.

173. SCOTTISH LEGAL BUILDING, 95 Bothwell St. 1927. *Wylie, Wright & Wylie*. Dignified 6-storey office block with shops on ground floor; Blaxter stone with cast iron infills below windows. Winner of an open competition. Sculpture by Archibald Dawson.

174

174. ST. JOHN'S RENFIELD CHURCH, 22 Beaconsfield Rd. 1929-31. *James Taylor Thomson.* Winner of an architectural competition in 1927. Makes good use of a rising site and something of a landmark on the western approach to Glasgow. Glass in main window by Douglas Strachan.

175. ST. MARGARET'S CHURCH, Knightswood Rd. 1925-32. *Sir Robert Lorimer & Matthew.* Simple round arched church with saddleback tower of Baltic inspiration. Notable interior woodwork.

176. COSMO CINEMA, Rose St. and Renfrew St. 1939. *W. J. Anderson II.* Small corner site well handled spacially; looks well from all angles. Steel frame; brickwork with some faience showing awareness of Dutch and Scandanavian practice. A decent and, for its time, a remarkably advanced building.

177

177. DAILY EXPRESS AND EVENING CITIZEN BUILDING, 163 Albion St. 1936. *Sir E. Owen Williams* of London. Similar in construction to the famous Boots' Factory at Beeston. Reinforced concrete frame faced in black glass with metal windows. A really twentieth-century looking newspaper office. An addition on the top uses same materials but is not so well proportioned.

178. READING ROOM, University of Glasgow, University Ave. 1939. *T. Harold Hughes & D. S. R. Waugh.* Provides accommodation for 400 students. Circular plan with central space for enquiries; book stacks extend to a lower floor. R.I B.A. Bronze Medal, 1949.

179. Cottages at Queen's Drive, near Queen's Park. 1950. *Glasgow Corporation Housing Department.* A pleasantly intimate group of cottages for old people. In 1951 the scheme won a Saltire Society award and a Festival of Britain award.

180. MOSS HEIGHTS, Cardonald. 1954. *Glasgow Corporation Housing Department*. Glasgow's first multi-storey housing scheme constructed of reinforced concrete with a cladding of aggregate precast concrete slabs.

181. Flats at Fyvie Avenue, Eastwood. 1951. *Glasgow Corporation Housing Department*. An example of well laid out 3-storey flats of a kind being built by the Corporation in the 1950s. Saltire award for the best designed flats completed in Scotland during 1951.

182. Flats at Crathie Drive, Partick. 1952. *Glasgow Corporation Housing Department*. This well sited block of flats for single people won still another success for Glasgow's public housing when it gained the Saltire Society's award for the best designed Scottish flats of 1952.

185. CRANHILL SECONDARY SCHOOL, 40 Startpoint St., nr. Edinburgh Rd. 1961. *Keppie, Henderson & J. L. Gleave*. Stands, well laid-out with playing fields, on a high incline overlooking the Edinburgh Rd; it has everything needed for modern secondary education, including a swimming pool. (*right*)

183. DEPARTMENT OF NATURAL PHILOSOPHY, University of Glasgow, Gilmorehill. 1951. *Basil Spence & Partners*. Perhaps the best recent addition to the group of buildings of various styles and periods that surround the main Gilbert Scott University (No. 88). 4-storey block clad in Portland stone; built to house research laboratories and an atom-splitting device, it contains heavy protective concrete and an intriguing moving floor. The same architects were responsible for the well-planned Institute of Virology, 1961, in nearby Church St. Other post-1945 Glasgow University buildings include those for Engineering (*Keppie, Henderson & J. L. Gleave*), Physical Education, Biochemistry, and Students' Amenity (all by *Keppie, Henderson & Partners*) and the Modern Languages Departments (*W. N. W. Ramsay*); others (see Nos. 218 and 219) are in the course of construction.

184. J. & T. BOYD'S TEXTILE MACH-INERY FACTORY, 219 Summerlee St. 1964. *Boswell, Mitchell & Johnston*. The Queenslie Industrial Estate, developed in the years following the Second World War, contains a number of cleanly designed modern factories. Boyd's is one of the best.

185

186. HIGHLAND HOUSE,
58 Waterloo St. 1959. *Michael Laird*
(Edinburgh). 7-storey office block
with 2-storey showroom. Reinforced
concrete structure with beamless flat
slab floors; modular planning to allow
internal flexibility; clad externally with
mosaic and engineering bricks.

187. TYPOGRAPHICAL HOUSE,
222 Clyde St. 1963. *Robert W. K. C.
Rogerson*. 4-storey office block for the
Typographical Society of Glasgow faced
with polished decorated precast concrete
slabs with contrasting black facing
bricks. Elevational treatment designed
to resist the grime of urban air.

188. DEPARTMENT OF PURE AND APPLIED CHEMISTRY,
University of Strathclyde, John St.-Cathedral St. corner. 1963. *Walter
Underwood & Partners*. Perhaps the most interesting of the recent additions
to the complex of buildings in the George St.-Cathedral St. area that
constitutes Glasgow's newly-established second University.

189. DAVID LIVINGSTONE TOWER, 94-168 George St. 1963. *Covell, Matthews & Partners*. Powerful building complex including a 17-storey irregularly shaped tower block in coloured curtain walling. Designed, as ALEC HOUSE, for commercial purposes, the upper storeys are now part of the University of Strathclyde.

190. CENTRAL COLLEGE OF COMMERCE AND DISTRIBUTION, 300 Cathedral St. 1963. *Wylie, Shanks & Partners*. Cosmopolitan style 7-storey building on rustic base; attractive entrance faced with travertine marble slabs; metal curtain walling with black infill panels.

191. GLASGOW COLLEGES OF BUILDING AND PRINTING, North Hanover St. and North Frederick St. 1964. *Wylie, Shanks & Partners*. A 12-storey building standing on an exposed concrete pilotis; reinforced concrete frame faced with travertine marble slabs on gables.

192. ST. ANDREWS HOUSE,
34 Sauchiehall St. 1964. *Arthur Swift &
Partners*. 2-storey podium surmounted by
15-storey office block. Reinforced concrete
frame with exposed aggregate cladding
panels; insistent vertical emphasis. A new
and powerful landmark in Sauchiehall Street.

193. ROYAL EXCHANGE ASSURANCE
HOUSE, 320 St. Vincent St. 1964. *Derek
Stephenson & Partners* (London). Ground
floor petrol station sharply divided from
main 8-storey office block by six-foot deep
podium clad in precast flint aggregate
panels; main office floors with spandrel wall
of handmade facing bricks.

194. LINN CREMATORIUM, Lainshaw Dr.
1962. *Thomas S. Cordiner*. Municipal
crematorium consisting of a main block
with side wings symmetrically placed about
a central axis; sited to command a view
over landscaped parkland.

192

193

195. WOLFSON HALL (University of
Glasgow), Garscube Estate, Maryhill Rd.
1964. *Building Design Partnership* (Preston).
Glasgow's first mixed hall of residence.
Main material grey brick; dominated by a
dramatic copper pyramidical roof over the
hall. Winner of a limited competition in 1960.

196. QUEEN MARGARET HALL
(University of Glasgow), between
Bellshaugh Rd. and Cleveden Gdns. 1964.
W. N. W. Ramsay. Women's hall replacing
Lilybank House (a 19-C. building with
Thomson additions in Gilmorehill area) now
used for University teaching. Two 4-storey
blocks of study-bedrooms linked by central
dining and common room area; concrete
frame exposed, with panels of brick and
timber. Extensions projected.

194

195

196

197. SCOTSTOUN FLATS.
Completed 1964. *A. G. Jury, City Architect and Director of Planning.*
A multi-storey housing scheme with Wimpey's as builders; no-fines concrete construction.

198. HUTCHESONTOWN-GORBALS REDEVELOPMENT: AREA B. 1962. *Robert Matthew, Johnson-Marshall & Partners* (Edinburgh). A dramatic mixed development on the banks of the Clyde consisting of four 17-storey housing blocks and lower buildings of three and four storeys.

199. HUTCHESONTOWN-GORBALS REDEVELOPMENT: AREA C. 1965. *Sir Basil Spence, Glover & Ferguson* (Edinburgh). A mixture of housing and shops. The slab blocks, containing 400 crossover maisonettes in each, have inter-connecting apartments and large balcony garden spaces.

200. POLLOKSHAWS DEVELOPMENT
AREA: UNIT 2, Shawbridge St. 1965.
Boswell, Mitchell & Johnston. A large
scale housing development; a mixture
of high (16 and 20 storeys) and low
(2 to 5 storeys) housing blocks arranged
to combine interesting interlocking
spaces with variety of view. The high
blocks constructed entirely of factory-
made concrete units.

201. LADYWELL HOUSING SCHEME,
Cathedral Sq. and Duke St. 1964.
Honeyman, Jack & Roberston. Three
15-storey tower blocks and a number of
lower buildings of 3 and 4 storeys; a
series of landscaped courtyards grouped
round the Drygate making good use of
a sloping site. Faced with stone on
Cathedral frontage; elsewhere, brick,
roughcast and concrete.

200

201

202. THE QUEEN MOTHER'S HOSPITAL, Yorkhill. 1964. *J. L. Gleave & Partners.* Adjoins J. J. Burnet's Royal Hospital for Sick Children. All ward accommodation on one floor with large tower block, dominating the group, containing living-in units.

203. ACCIDENT AND ORTHOPAEDIC DEPART-MENT, Southern General Hospital, Govan Rd. 1964. *Keppie, Henderson & Partners.* Simple, well laid-out addition to existing 19-C. hospital; first large post-war unit of its kind in Scotland and therefore something of a model.

204. ST. MARTIN'S R.C. CHURCH, 201 Ardencraig Rd., Castlemilk. 1963. *Gillespie, Kidd & Coia.* One of a group of well-designed churches by these architects in and around Glasgow (see No. 206). Well integrated composition set on a steep and rocky site; approached by a series of steps and terraces.

205. ST. CHRISTOPHER'S CHURCH, Meikle Rd. 1961-62. *A. Buchanan Campbell.* Church of Scotland Extension Church; facing brick and weatherboard exterior; floor to ceiling windows lighting the sanctuary.

206. ST. CHARLES' R.C. CHURCH, 1 Kelvinside Gdns. 1960. *Gillespie, Kidd & Coia.* Elegantly-planned church, accommodating 900, dominated by 80 ft. free-standing tower. Exposed concrete frame with infill panels of rustic facing bricks and aluminium screen. Interior with subtly vaulted concrete ceiling. Sculpture includes Stations of the Cross by Benno Schotz.

207. HUTCHESONS' BOYS' GRAMMAR SCHOOL, Beaton Rd. 1957-60. *Boswell, Mitchell & Johnston*. New building, in contemporary idiom, which does something to translate the history and traditions of a long established foundation.

208. KING'S PARK SECONDARY SCHOOL, 6 Fetlar Dr., Castlemilk. 1964. *Gillespie, Kidd & Coia*. For 1350 pupils. On a steeply sloping site with a dominating 4-storey double cantilever classroom block; this and the 2-storey blocks are of reinforced concrete construction.

209. ST. FRANCIS PRIMARY SCHOOL FOR BOYS, Hutcheson Sq. 1963. *J. L. Gleave & Partners*. Compactly planned 3-storey classroom block with detached infant block. Pre-cast concrete with some load bearing brick walls; facing brick panel infill lower storeys, architect-designed timber and steel curtain wall cladding two upper storeys.

210. EASTMUIR PRIMARY SCHOOL, 211 Halihill Rd., Barlanark. 1963. *Boswell, Mitchell & Johnston*. School for handicapped children intimately placed in pleasant woodland setting. The nearby Woodcroft School and Garthamlock Secondary School are by the same architects.

211. OUR LADY AND ST. FRANCIS SECONDARY SCHOOL: ANNEXE, Charlotte St. by Glasgow Green. 1964. *Gillespie, Kidd & Coia*. Reinforced concrete frame; metal windows with infill panels. Attractive treatment of street elevations. One of an interesting group of works by these architects.

212. BARMULLOCH COLLEGE OF FURTHER EDUCATION, 186 Rye Rd. 1964. *D. Harvey, A. Scott & Associates*. Blocks of varying height combine contemporary composition and detailing with a straightforward solution of a common problem; interesting tiled feature panels.

213. JORDANHILL COLLEGE: NEW BUILDINGS, Southbrae Dr. 1962-3. *Keppie, Henderson & Partners*. Extensions to an old Victorian style (begun 1914!) college. A large refectory, a 25m. swimming pool, a 4,400 sq. ft. games hall and a music and drama tutorial building. (*above*)

214. ANNIESLAND COLLEGE OF FURTHER EDUCATION, Hatfield Dr. 1964. *Ross, Doak & Whitelaw*. 4-storey teaching block, single storey workshop and community blocks; exposed reinforced concrete with facing brick panel infill at ground floor level. (*centre*)

215. LANGSIDE COLLEGE, 23 Valeview Terr. 1965. *Boissevain & Osmond*. Further Education college; winning design in an open competition. Crisp interpretation of contemporary idiom interestingly constructed of square steel tubes and steel curtain walling. Set on a hillside, there are five different levels. (*left*)

216. ROYAL STUART HOTEL, Clyde St. and Jamaica St. 1965. *Walter Underwood & Partners.* Spacious hotel, completely air-conditioned, overlooking the Clyde; shops on ground floor; basement car park; reinforced concrete frame clad in mosaic.

217. TINTO FIRS HOTEL, 470 Kilmarnock Rd. 1964. *T. M. Miller.* Rooms grouped round an internal patio. Good example of a small hotel in contemporary architectural idiom. Makes an interesting contrast with the surrounding stone-built villas.

The
Future

The appearance of Glasgow is changing rapidly. In the face of so much activity it is impossible to give even systematic coverage to future architectural projects, and we must be content with sampling the main lines of development : buildings for higher education, commercial buildings, and two schemes to illustrate the Corporation's Redevelopment Plan. These must stand as representatives for many other projects of equal interest. They are of necessity here illustrated from models.

The centrepiece of the new Glasgow University buildings rising above Gilmorehill will be the UNIVERSITY LIBRARY AND ART GALLERY (No. 218) by *William Whitfield* of London. The core of the building is 11 storeys but the architect has brought the vertical services out in a number of towers which project above the roof-line to a maximum height of some 160 ft., forming a dramatic composition reminiscent of San Gimignano, which is intended to complement the University spire across the road. The lower blocks in the foreground contain, besides the new Gallery, the Fine Art Department and a reconstruction of the Mackintosh house from Southpark Avenue (see No. 149).

A little further to the west is the half-complete ADAM SMITH BUILDING (No. 219) by *Harvey, Scott & Associates*, which is to provide accommodation for the Social Science Departments. It is finished, like the Library, in pre-cast flint aggregate panels, but sets these off strikingly against large areas of glass.

The third main building on the Gilmorehill site, to the east of the Library, is the STUDENTS' REFECTORY BUILDING by *Frank Fielden & Associates* ; his building for his own SCHOOL OF ARCHITECTURE at the University of Strathclyde (No. 220) is perhaps even more interesting. It is set back in a court off Rotten Row. The necessity of avoiding direct light in the studios in the upper storeys, which are lit by north light from the roof, has led to an interesting pattern of blind projecting bays on the south elevation, with windows in the reveals. The finish is in blue engineering brick and fair-faced concrete.

218

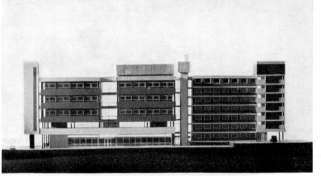

219

220

221

Also for the University of Strathclyde, *Sir Robert Matthew, Johnson-Marshall & Partners* are building a METALLURGY LABORATORY (No. 221) adjoining the old Royal College building. This consists of heavy laboratories in the three-storey base, with lecture rooms in a further four storeys at the western end; further additions are planned. The finish is of white tile, with vitreous enamelled panels.

The EXTENSION FOR THE GLASGOW SCHOOL OF ART (No. 222) by *Keppie, Henderson & Partners* is being built in several phases along Renfrew Street from east to west. The first phase is already built. The second, a seven-storey tower which was a requirement of the Fine Arts Commission, is conceived as the east side of a courtyard facing the Mackintosh building (see No. 146) to the south; the finish of grey sandstock brick is designed to complement it in texture (in the photograph, the rendering of the tower is misleading in this respect). The western parts of the courtyard are still under discussion.

The seven-storey office block on St. Vincent St. and Wellington St. (No. 223) by *Wylie, Shanks & Partners* is an example of the better kind of office block now being built in the centre of Glasgow. The facing is of dark brick, and the podium, which conceals a basement garage, is of white Carrara marble. The recessed frontage not only makes good use of the narrow site but creates a space in which the strong verticals of the bay window and narrow service tower can dominate the street corner without cutting out the light.

Systematic development in the centre of Glasgow is dealt with in the Corporation's concept of Comprehensive Development Areas. Eight areas, roughly encircling the city-centre—Woodside, Cowcaddens, Townhead, Royston, Glasgow Cross, Hutchesontown/Gorbals, Laurieston/Gorbals, Shields Road and Anderston Cross—have been designated for redevelopment over the next 20 years. The Plan includes lower density housing, shopping, offices, entertainment and recreational centres and, in certain areas, industrial development. The eight areas are to be linked by a new ring road (part of which can be seen in No. 225A). *Jack Holmes & Partners* have prepared an extensive scheme for an INDUSTRIAL ZONE in ANDERSTON CROSS C. D. A. (No. 224A). This consists of a number of flatted factory blocks rising out of two superimposed decks which cover the whole area of the site. These are connected by ramps and provide vehicular access to the factory loading bays and goods lifts. The streets are thus kept free and, functional concerns apart, the visual isolation of the entire complex should be very impressive (No. 224B).

222

223

224A

224B

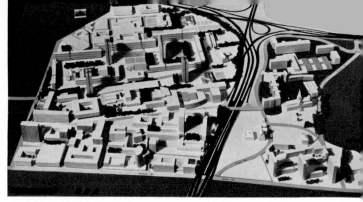

225A

The appearance of TOWNHEAD C. D. A. (No. 225A) is already being altered by the building programme of Strathclyde University in its southern section. The photograph shows how the zone is comparatively quiet, the traffic being diverted around by the ring road. This concept of the area as a quiet enclave is reinforced by the layout of the principal residential area (No. 225B) which uses linked seven-storey blocks to form a series of planted piazzas punctuated by the point blocks — the advantage of multi-storey housing being that land can be released for recreational purposes in this way. The scheme was prepared by *A. G. Jury, C.B.E.,* who, as City Architect, is responsible for the whole Redevelopment plan. The commission for a new precinct for the Cathedral, to the east of Townhead, has been given to *Sir William Holford.*

These are just a few of the works in progress. There are others soon to be started including Mr. Jury's scheme for the new St. Andrew's Halls. New building on this scale will without doubt make great changes to the social conditions of Glasgow. It will also have the power of enhancing the city's appearance by providing new architecture that is worthy of, and in harmony with, the best of the old.

225B

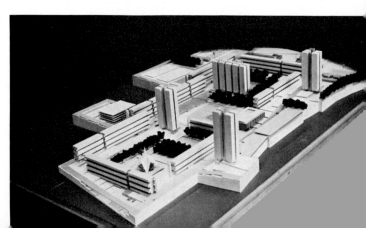

Index of Architects

Index of Buildings and Streets

Addendum : John Brash is now known to be the architect of Blythswood Square, **24**